JACKIE

JACKIE

I Did It My Way

Jackie Fullerton
with Roger Anderson

MAINSTREAM
PUBLISHING
EDINBURGH AND LONDON

First published in Great Britain in 2006 by
MAINSTREAM PUBLISHING COMPANY
(EDINBURGH) LTD
7 Albany Street
Edinburgh EH1 3UG

ISBN 1 84596 085 8

A catalogue record for this book is available
from the British Library

Typeset in Baskerville and Din

Printed in Great Britain by
William Clowes Ltd, Beccles, Suffolk

Jackie's dedication

In memory of my parents, Martha and Jack, who enriched and influenced my life in so many ways.

Roger's dedication

For my wife, Pamela, and daughters, Amy, Hannah and Ellie.

ACKNOWLEDGEMENTS

The first of many people I have to thank is my biographer and BBC colleague, Roger Anderson. Over a year ago, Roger declared, 'I want to talk to you about your favourite subject – you!' Not totally factual but a strong selling point that has seen him burn the midnight oil listening to my rantings captured on tape. Roger has kept the tapes – he assures me he will never suffer from insomnia again. Seriously, Roger has worked long hours on the book, so I apologise to his wife, Pamela, and their three daughters for stealing him away from normal family life.

I also pay tribute to my own wife, Linda. A strong and loving supporter, she has guided me through the highs and lows of the often precarious business of television. Our three sons, Darren, Nicolas and Gareth, have my thanks for their love and support. They and Linda also deserve credit for jogging memories of our life together.

I am indebted to my Ballymena friend James Nesbitt for his kind foreword. He seemed reluctant to write it, but when I said, 'It's either you or Sir Alex,' our Jimmy came around to my way of thinking. I also want to mention my mate, and Northern Ireland Press Photographer of the Year, William Cherry, who took the photograph that adorns the front cover. Thanks, William. Just how long did the airbrushing take? Sincere thanks are also due to Bill Campbell at Mainstream Publishing for believing in the project, to Claire Rose for her meticulous editing and to designer Emily Bland for her excellent work on the jacket.

Jackie Fullerton

CONTENTS

FOREWORD

I was about nine or ten years old when I first met Jackie. My Uncle Bertie, a reporter with one of the local newspapers, took me along to an Irish League game at Ballymena Showgrounds. This was an era before wall-to-wall television coverage of football, when kids my age regarded a trip to the Warden Street ground as a Saturday treat and, to us, a player like Ballymena United's midfielder Arthur Stewart assumed *galáctico* status. That's why I was just a little awestruck when Uncle Bertie took me into the United dressing-room before kick-off. Clutching an autograph book in my clammy hands and with the smell of liniment in my nostrils, I tagged along as my uncle introduced me to Arthur and the other members of the team. It was just as we were about to leave that Uncle stopped to speak to this sharp-dressed chap. 'James,' he said, looking down at me, 'this is Jackie, he does the sport on the telly.'

For blokes of my generation, Jackie Fullerton became the very embodiment of local sport. 'League leaders Linfield . . .', the introduction delivered with Lynam-like smoothness, is an instantly recognisable opening gambit we bandied about the school corridor. Jackie was our link to local sport, the man who brought a little bit of show business to the nightly news. His verbal sparring in the studio with Gloria [Hunniford], the night Giant Haystacks threw him to the ground like a rag doll, those countless consummate international commentaries: Jackie became a part of the fixtures and fittings. We knew he came with credibility. I can still picture him in the red-and-black stripes of Crusaders, peering out from that League Championship-winning photograph UTV wheeled out at every opportunity. We knew he liked to sing – I mean Christmas wouldn't have been complete without his customary crooning.

Like so many people, I was genuinely upset when I heard about Jackie's illness in 2004. It came as a real shock. What wasn't surprising, though, was the warmth extended to him by a public that has really taken him to their hearts. We've all come to regard Jackie as the very essence of local sport, the polished professional who educates, illuminates and entertains. I was delighted when he returned to Old Trafford for the World Cup qualifier between England and Northern Ireland, even more so that Jackie was the man behind the mike on that wonderful night in September 2005 when David Healy's strike beat Beckham and the boys. I'm pretty sure my old autograph book's still kicking around my dad's house somewhere. It's not often I get the opportunity to leaf through its pages, but when I do it still makes me proud when I turn the page and see the fading signatures of that Ballymena United team and Jackie. After all, it's not every day you get to meet your sporting heroes *and* your hero off the television.

James Nesbitt, May 2006

FROM THE HEART

Love was in very short supply around the Luis Casanova Stadium. Any affection the home supporters had been willing to extend to little old Northern Ireland was swept away two minutes into the second half when Gerry Armstrong slammed the ball into the Spanish net. A single swing of the big man's right boot was all it took to transform eardrum-perforating passion into stunned silence, as if the mute button had been pressed on some giant remote control. The stadium paused, a split second of agony before ecstasy. I was trapped, along with the Northern Ireland players and the small pocket of travelling supporters, in what felt like a collective moment of self-doubt. None of us, I think, could quite believe we'd scored. Then it hit us. The roar trapped in the fans' throats did escape, and the players did celebrate. For me, though, that instant would have to be about suppressed emotions. Sitting pitch-side, behind the goal opposite the one in which the ball nestled, I was close enough to feel Spanish supporters' breath on the back of my neck. I wanted to jump up, to punch the air, but self-preservation took over. No point in showing a red rag to a bull.

If England's seminal football moment in '66 has one clear advantage over Northern Ireland's in '82, it's that it was indeed 'all over' after Sir Geoff's strike. For us, big Gerry's goal only kick-started the most excruciating clock-watch imaginable. We buried our heads in our hands when, ten minutes after we'd taken the lead, Paraguayan referee Hector Ortiz controversially sent Mal Donaghy for an early bath. We fumed as, time and again, scything Spanish tackles went unpunished. We agonised as wave after wave of attacks foundered on a defence marshalled by the majestic Pat Jennings. We kicked every ball, made every tackle and headed every clearance. Hell, we were all ready for the funny farm as it trickled into injury time.

The second hand seemed to slow as my heart rate increased. I exchanged glances with my colleague from ITV, Elton Welsby. From our vantage point in the pocket of a couple of thousand angry Spaniards, we tried our best to remain impartial and professional. Elton wasn't from Northern Ireland, but he'd developed a genuine soft spot for Billy Bingham's boys during his stay in the team hotel. For me, of course, it ran much deeper than that. I fluctuated from fan to broadcaster and back again. I prayed for the torment to end. Finally, it did. A shrill blast and the realisation: 'My God! We've won!' Elton and I embraced and then immediately focused on the job in hand. We needed interviews. It was agreed: I would grab the goal-scorer, Gerry Armstrong; he would nab the skipper, Martin O'Neill. I set off running.

If I ever need reminding about the conclusion to my pitch invasion in Valencia that night, I can always dig out a video of ITV's World Cup coverage. There, in the opening titles, is a shot of three demented souls hugging like long-lost brothers in the centre circle. It was Billy Bingham, Gerry Armstrong and a wee man from Ballymena with a blue shirt and white collar (I swear it was the fashion at the time). Billy and Gerry had tears in their eyes, and I had a lump in my throat like the widow at a wake. Emotional? Hell, yes! And why not? I mean, it wasn't supposed to happen like this. In fact, it hadn't since Peter Doherty's side shook the world in Sweden 24 years earlier. That was the era of Gregg, Peacock, Blanchflower, McIlroy and McParland, when a wide-eyed teenager from Ballymena walked across the Railway Bridge to see the stars strut their stuff at Windsor Park. Now that boy from the country was witnessing at close quarters the birth of a whole new generation of football heroes. If there was a next best thing to actually playing, well, surely this was it.

Fast-forward more than two decades. The Millennium Stadium in Cardiff is the setting for another World Cup roller-coaster ride with Northern Ireland. Palpitations again for me and every other 'Norn Iron' supporter as we conspire to lose a two-goal lead, two players prematurely exit stage left and we hang on for a dramatic draw. It was the following morning, just as I was checking in at the airport, that I felt the first twinge. I wouldn't call it a pain in my chest, more a feeling of discomfort. It's hard to describe, but it just didn't feel right. I'm not a brave man in situations like this, and denial is usually the first course of action. So I made a mental note to see about the problem when I got home. I did go for a check-up, but, as is often the case, there wasn't so much as a twinge to report. That is, until Tuesday, 14 September 2004. I remember the date not just because of the significance it would later assume but because it's two days after the birthday of my sister Mareen (an abbreviation of 'Mary Roberta'). That was the evening the strange, suffocating sensation in my chest came back with a vengeance. Only this time it didn't disappear. Heart bypass surgery would follow in the coming days, a terrifying yet strangely life-affirming experience.

Life is full of the unexpected. Fortunately, for me, the

highs have far outweighed the lows. I had a childhood characterised by song and smiles, and a successful playing career in Irish League football that brought me into contact, often literally, with some of the game's genuine characters. Then came the break into television. It was a gentleman by the name of Sydney Perry, controller of Ulster Television, who gave me my start on the small screen, and a word of warning: 'Eventually, when you get over your nerves, the real you will shine through. If it doesn't, the viewer will spot it a mile away.'

Nearly half of my 63 years have been spent peering out at the public from a box in the corner of their living-rooms. They've got to know me, although the signals have sometimes become confused. What is, I hope, a smooth studio delivery has metamorphosed into the 'Mr Smooth' image. Often grossly exaggerated, it's got so bad I've even started impersonating myself, a bizarre and mildly disturbing development. In the end, there's nothing I can do about people who think that if I were chocolate, I'd eat myself. The majority of folk, I'm pleased to say, appear to like what they see. The rapport I have with the man and woman in the street means the world to me, from the good-natured banter with the terrace wags to the punters who still shout, 'What about Giant Haystacks?' and, of course, those tongue-in-cheek demands for me to sing. My media career has also afforded me the opportunity of witnessing at first hand some great sporting moments and of meeting the men and women who made them happen. I can say, hand on heart, that my heroes have, by and large, lived up to expectations. Some, like George Best and Joey Dunlop, far exceeded them.

It's been quite a journey, and if laughter can be used as a life barometer, then I've not done too badly. I've been entertained and hopefully done my share of entertaining. And, sure, I may have polished a few of the rough edges over the years, but underneath I remain that working-class lad from Ballymena's Harryville housing estate. This is my story, from the heart, my way.

Chapter One

PRAMS, PISTOLS AND PAN-AIDA

I couldn't wait for the bell to ring. I had to get home. There was no time to lose. On any other weekday afternoon, the first port of call would have been a kickabout on the 'wee park', but not today. I burst through the front door, quickly confirmed that no one was home and raced upstairs. Before you could say 'Superman in a phone box', my school uniform was on the floor and I was standing in front of the bedroom mirror in socks and shorts. Now was the time. I slowly unfolded the royal-blue shirt. Then, without even so much as a ceremonial drum roll to mark the occasion, I pulled it over my head. It dropped. I thought it would never stop. Past my waist it went, past my shorts, calling a halt just above my kneecaps. The section that was expecting to find itself filled by my shoulders slumped instead to just above my elbow. There was such a mass of material it made me look like the boy with the incredible shrunken head. And do you know what? I didn't care. Nothing could spoil the moment. For this was no ordinary shirt. This was the one handed to me a few hours earlier by Mr Will Moore, full-time teacher and part-time football coach at Harryville School. Possession signified team selection. It meant that this scrawny nine year old was going to get his chance to play with the big boys. Of course, I would have to develop a novel system of folding and tucking to ensure the shirt wouldn't trip me up when I ran – but it was a small price to pay.

I suppose it would be fair to say football is in the blood. My father played for Ballymena United in the Irish League before the Second World War interrupted his career. Like hundreds of other players, he put aside his football boots and took up arms, seeing action in North Africa, Sicily and Italy with the Royal Inniskilling Fusiliers. It was an experience that affected him deeply. Though he never talked about the conflict, it didn't take a psychologist to tell us he'd been scarred by the horrors of war. It certainly stripped him of any tolerance for triviality. Happy and humorous most of the time, he could nonetheless fly into a rage when faced with frivolous conversation. It was almost as if he felt guilty indulging in idle chitchat, that somehow it belittled the enormous sacrifices made by friends left behind on foreign fields.

It was during Dad's wartime furlough in 1942 that he and my mother decided to add to the ranks of the Fullerton family. Sure enough, on 22 May 1943, just five days after those famously destructive Dambuster raids, a bouncing baby boy was born in the Waveney Hospital, Ballymena. The proud parents, John and Martha Fullerton, didn't deliberate over names for long. Like his father, and *his* father before, the lad would be christened John Alexander. For the first few years after the war, you could say it was cosy, what with me, my elder brother, Jimmy, our parents and grandparents all sharing the upstairs attic of 41 Queen Street – a house in Ballymena's Harryville district owned by the railway. Space, like most other things post-war, was in short supply. Of course, a little privacy could always be secured with a brief excursion to the igloo that posed as our outside toilet. It wasn't much warmer indoors, but at least ingenuity was in plentiful supply. Jimmy and I slept soundly in the bed we shared at night, thanks to a cumbersome combination of blankets, coats and eiderdowns (that's duvets to the cultured folk of today). This layering effect would have kept Hillary warm on Everest; it also required the strength of an Olympic weightlifter to get out of bed in the morning.

There's always the fear that with the passing years you begin to view childhood through rose-tinted spectacles. But I can say, hand on heart, that I don't ever recall being hungry, cold or in any way deprived. Perhaps the credit should go to my parents for protecting us from the world outside, for ensuring we were provided for at a time when paucity was par for the course. It was an uncomplicated era, when simple pleasures like a bag of sweets could leave you grinning from ear to ear.

The 'sweet emporium', as my young aunt, June Hamill, Jimmy and I called the converted front parlour of Martha Graham's house, was our equivalent of Willy Wonka's Chocolate Factory. From there, this shrewd old lady dispensed all things sticky and sweet to an entire neighbourhood. Rationing was still in operation and military precision sometimes required to break down Martha's defences. That's when the family wheeled out their secret weapon. On those occasions when A, B and C coupons had been used well ahead of schedule, little Jack was sent for. Working on the premise that no one could refuse an angelic five year old, I was charged with swapping D coupons for quarters of sweets. It was seldom quite as straightforward as all that. Certainly, you could never accuse Martha of short-changing you in the entertainment department. Before you got your hands on the sweets, she invariably produced a performance of Oscar-winning proportions. First, she would feign annoyance that she should be asked such a thing, then she'd lecture strongly on the illegality of the entire process and finally she would find it in her heart to fill those small, white paper bags.

Well, if it worked for sweets why not go the whole hog, so to speak? So I was also regularly dispatched to another of our swap-shops, Connon's the butcher. In exchange for a bucket of the Fullerton's potato peelings (ideal pig feed), Mrs Connon would drop a penny into my clammy claws. Within seconds of copper touching flesh, I was off in the direction of Eddie Maternaghan's grocer shop, and before that penny had a chance to singe my pocket, it was swapped for four apples and a couple of chews. Then off down Queen Street I'd trot, happy as a pig in the proverbial.

I'm aware that, on occasions, my reminiscences make me sound like an extra from a *Monty Python* sketch. You know, the one where the flat-capped Englishmen tell increasingly exaggerated tales of the hardships they endured growing up. Well, I was never forced to walk home from school through the snow in my bare feet, but there's one thing the *Python* boys were right about: you tell the young people of today about life back then, and they just don't believe you. Take my sons, Darren, Nicky and Gareth. They regard it as a running joke when I parade out sepia-toned stories of prams, pistols and pan-aida. 'Not the one about the pram again,' they say, when I tell them about the home-made one their grandfather crafted for their mother, minus a hood because the money for it ran out. 'Not that old chestnut about the Christmas present,' they groan, when I recount how happy we were to get a toy gun at Christmas – no holster, just the gun. And let's not forget that favourite tasty tale I reserve for family outings to the restaurant. Pan-aida was served up to us as kids as a treat. Pan bread cut into squares, soaked in a bowl of milk and sprinkled with sugar, it was eaten at breakfast, or for that matter supper. If the folks were really pushing the boat out, the milk was heated. My kids can, of course, set their watches by me casually perusing the menu before announcing, 'I think I'll start with the pan-aida.'

Everyone, I suppose, would like to say they had an idyllic childhood. In reality, growing up, like being a grown-up, brings its fair share of ups and downs. There was a stage when you could have plied me with 20 bowls of the best pan-aida and I still wouldn't have gone to school. To be honest, my education didn't really get off to the best of starts. Actually, I was six when I had my first formal lesson at Guy's School on Wellington Street. Within days, I decided enough was enough and walked out. My bid for freedom didn't last for too long, though, thanks to Charlie Beattie. He recognised me in the street (Charlie, like our family, attended the local Methodist church) and rightly figured I should be somewhere else. As a bank messenger, he was required to wear a black uniform topped off by a natty peaked cap. To your average six-year-old runaway, he looked just like a policeman. My desperado days over, I went quietly, and Charlie calmly led me by the hand back to class. It's ironic that, two years later, transferring from Guy's to Harryville School should be so traumatic. For the first four months in the new school, I would have done anything to return to the place I once couldn't wait to leave.

The trouble with Harryville School came in human form, and it began virtually from the moment I walked into my third-year class. From the very outset, the teacher seemed determined to give me a rough ride. With hindsight, I reckon her behaviour towards me was well-intentioned, it's just I didn't see it that way at the time. She attended our church, knew who I was, yet refused to cut me any slack. I was struggling to adjust to the lessons and my new surroundings, but my teacher could only see lack of effort. I was finding my inadequacies embarrassing in front of my new classmates, but sympathy was in short supply. Maybe her tough tactics were designed to motivate me. They had the opposite effect. Soon, I was trying every trick in the book to stay off school. Occasionally, it worked. I think my mum could sense there was more to this than met the eye, and every now and again I was allowed Friday afternoon off. Term finally ended. So did my torment. When I returned, it was to a new teacher. I had moved up to fourth grade and Jim Soutar's class. Unlike my previous teacher and I, we got on like a house on fire. Jim was a wonderful teacher and a wonderful man. I blossomed under his tender tutelage.

I was always a mummy's boy, I suppose. She understood me, and I in turn worshipped the ground she walked on. As a family, we were fairly typical of the time. Dad, as the man of the house, ruled the roost. A bus driver, it's a tribute to his strong work ethic that even when employment was hard to come by, he always managed to earn a wage. He had his frailties, too. He got drunk occasionally and, like most men, enjoyed a bet. The latter vice caused more friction at home than the former. I can recall a few occasions when Dad blew his entire week's wage on a sure thing that proved anything but. Maybe the bookie's shop was a form of escapism, those few brief moments as the horses careered between the fences the closest Dad got to an adrenalin rush. However, when gambling deprived the family of groceries, my mum certainly didn't hold back. Voices were raised, but those disputes were seldom anything other than short-lived, between a man and woman who clearly loved each other dearly.

If Dad's foible was a pointless punt on some daft three-legged nag, Mum's was undoubtedly working-class pride. It manifested itself in her refusal to admit we had lived in Slemish Drive, prefabricated housing first erected in 1948. Wee Martha just couldn't quite get over the stigma attached to prefabs. She tried her best to wipe away the memory of the two years we spent there. In fact, if ever Jimmy and I brought

21 Slemish Drive into conversation, Mum would quickly correct us, substituting nearby Warden Street. I don't recall there being anything actually wrong with the prefabs, but if it made her happy then we were happy to oblige.

If that short tenure at the 'top o' the town', as it was known, was a problem for Mum, it presented no such predicament to me. You see, Slemish Drive was just a stone's throw from Ballymena Showgrounds. This meant that on any given Saturday, a young lad only had to bide his time until someone took pity and lifted him over the wall. With no tabloids or television to track a footballer's every move, this was the only chance you got to see your heroes. Supporters would congregate outside the dressing-rooms, straining for a glimpse of men like Johnny Morrison, the dashing winger, Joe Douglas, a balding wing-half who had played for Belfast Celtic, or Johnny and Sammy Mitten, brothers of Manchester United star Charlie.

And we fans wouldn't even take time to relax at half-time. During the interval and again after the final whistle, we would all try our hand at being a Morrison, Douglas or Mitten. On the Showgrounds back pitch used by Ballymena Rugby Club before their move to Eaton Park, supporters would take part in impromptu kickabouts. These 50-a-side scrummages could, not surprisingly, be physical encounters, with the poor ball suffering the most punishment. Jimmy and I found that out the hard way. One Saturday, the Fullerton brothers made the mistake of taking along the shiny new plastic ball their mother had splashed out on for her boys. I suppose we brought it hoping to impress the massed ranks. Sadly, ten minutes at half-time was all it took to burst our bubble, and the ball.

The best lessons are often the ones that are the hardest to learn – something I would continue to find. Thankfully, in my football education at least, I was fortunate to have mentors who had already seen it, done it and boasted the

T-shirt at home. Take the Intermediate School football team. Our coach was none other than Hubert Barr, then a player with Ballymena United. Hubert would go on to be part of Linfield's seven-trophy-winning team, alongside Tommy 'The Duke' Dickson, before moving to Coventry City. He was also capped for Northern Ireland in a 1–1 draw with England at Wembley in 1961. Hubert imparted pearls of wisdom at school, while at Harryville Presbyterian Boys' Brigade (there was no Boys' Brigade in my own church at the time) it was another Showgrounds star who passed on advice. For in addition to the local battalion's captain, Stanley McIlroy, and officers Maurice Grant and Alex Richardson, we had local hero Willie Cubitt. Willie was an icon to us lads, having played in the Ballymena United side that beat Linfield 2–0 at The Oval in the 1958 Irish Cup final. Despite their wealth of experience, however, there were occasions when neither Hubert nor Willie could prevent reality kicking in.

My father used to say I was 'built like a bicycle pump', and sure enough I was small for my age. On the plus side, I had a decent left foot, close control and, for a winger, an eye for a goal. I recall scoring in a 3–1 win for the Intermediate over Four Towns, from Ahoghill, in the final of the O'Kane Cup. We were so pleased with ourselves that the entire team walked from the Phoenix Grounds to the house of our headmaster, Billy Holmes, just to break the news of our victory. Unfortunately, we were soon to become the victims of our own success. The next step was a trip to the city to play Ashfield School. It didn't take long for us to realise we had been merely big fish in a small pond, as the city team thumped us 6–0. It was the first time, although definitely not the last, that I would feel intimidated by the bigger and more streetwise boys from Belfast.

A few years later, an incident during a match for Ballymena United Reserves reminded me that I was still very much a raw country boy with a not-so-healthy inferiority complex. We were up against a Linfield Swifts side that included in the starting XI Billy Ferguson. Billy, who was returning from injury, was one of the leading players in the Irish League (he would later be capped by Northern Ireland). There was a hold-up in play, and I started some eye-catching ball juggling, I suppose trying to impress Billy. It didn't work. Just as the referee blew his whistle to restart the match, Billy looked over at me with total disdain and hollered, 'Hey, Pelé! Give us the f***ing ball!' All I could muster in retort was to do exactly as he asked and then stand there looking sheepish. There was one consolation. Just as defeat to Ashfield had been made bearable by the fact that the game was staged at Celtic Park (a stadium I'd heard my father and uncles talk about in tones of hushed reverence), so this embarrassing episode was offset by a first-ever appearance on Windsor Park's famous sward.

If the odd battering in Belfast brought me down to earth, it was handsomely supplemented a little closer to home. For a 16 year old who seldom strayed far beyond his own age group, the Ballymena Junior League was a whole new world. 'Junior' was in fact a real misnomer. It was sink-or-swim time, and I had David Cairns to thank for forcing me to take the plunge. We had first met at the Boys' Brigade, and like so many of the friendships forged during that time in my life, ours would last a lifetime. Bertie Thompson and Maurice 'Mousey' Falls, Brian Blackadder (who would later be best man at my wedding), his younger brother Ian, Francis Smith, Harold Torbitt, Bobby McCaig, Uel 'Luggy' Allen, Carson Crawford, Alan and Joe Kyle – they became an extension of my family. None more so than David, who arrived at my front door one Saturday morning bursting with the news that he'd got me a game with Hillview. For both of us, this was a real step up, a chance to impress. It was Hillview versus Lisnafillan, and I only had to wander out onto the pitch to realise that this was as far away from Boys' Brigade or school football as you could get. Some of these guys looked like they'd kick their grannies just to get at us. I didn't have long to wait for my introduction. Early in the match, the ball was pushed along the left wing. There was plenty of time to cross before the defender closed me down. Or so I thought. The ball was long gone, but the full-back just kept on coming. I ended up kicking the bottom of his studs as he followed through. That sharp twist of pain was accompanied by the realisation that this was not a place for the faint-hearted. Pathé newsreels might have given me the impression that in the 'beautiful game' defenders stood back and admired the skills of Matthews and Finney, but this was an infinitely uglier arena. Later in the evening, nursing my fat and discoloured foot, it dawned on me that I had no option but to shape up or ship out.

If winter was almost exclusively about football, save the odd fool notion about taking up boxing (I was briefly inspired by Randolph Turpin's shock win over the legendary middleweight Sugar Ray Robinson in July 1951), then summer saw a sizeable share of my leisure time spent at the crease. My interest in cricket was nurtured from an early age by my uncle, Alex Hamill. Fancied himself as a bit of a spin bowler, did my uncle. In fact, he thought he was Ballymena's answer to Sonny Ramadhin, the West Indian star of the time. Together we would recreate tense Test matches in the alley alongside my Queen Street home. Funny, a couple of years ago during a 12th of July parade I inadvertently found myself on Queen Street. Maybe it was the smell of summer that lingered in the air that day, but I couldn't help reminiscing about that path we transformed into Trent Bridge and The Oval. I couldn't resist a peek. Time can play tricks on the mind, though, and I was genuinely surprised to find it barely big enough to swing a cat, let alone a cricket bat. How small I must have been to find such restrictive boundaries believable.

Cricket continued to play an important part in my summers for many years to come; leather on willow (or in our case rock-hard sponge ball on willow) was the soundtrack to our holidays. On one occasion, however, that familiar sound was quickly followed by a sharper and more worrying noise. My mates and I were playing in 'the square', as we called the space near my Chichester Park home. I was batting. More than that, I was in the zone. It was so easy, hell, he could have been bowling a beach ball. I saw it early and swung. Up it went, a six from the moment it left my bat. How Richie Benaud would have revelled in describing that strike! Although I'm not sure how he would have handled the ball smashing its way through a neighbour's front window and onto the carpet of his living-room. All I could think about as I shuffled towards Jackie Tennant's front door was the reception my father would lay on for me when he found out. To this day, I don't know why Jackie decided to be quite so magnanimous – I mean, it was the biggest window in the house and money was scarce. But he just said, 'Son, I'm sure you didn't mean it. Don't worry about it.' And he never did tell my dad.

From sticky wickets to the sticky, energy-sapping pitches of the Junior League, they were great days, and a great foundation. Eventually, though, I was going to have to look beyond the confines of Ballymena. With my 18th birthday approaching, I began playing for Bangor Reserves. It proved to be an ideal stepping stone, one that would actually hasten my move into the middle of those same city folk who once so intimidated me. I settled quickly at Clandeboye Road, scoring regularly for Bangor's second string. Back in my home town, Joe McCall nodded his approval. Joe had watched me emerge from the Junior League; now he felt it was time to move onwards and upwards. He recommended me to Glentoran, and, clearly valuing his opinion, the East Belfast outfit asked me to sign on the dotted line. By day, I worked for the Irish

Bonding Company, moving into digs on Glenvarlock Street, off the Castlereagh Road. By night, I trained with the Glens' third team under the watchful eye of Bud McFarland, a man who had been one of the early influences on George Best's career. My landlord, Reggie Clarke, and his family (wife Margaret and daughter Helen) made adjusting to life in the city so much easier; and I was soon getting my feet well and truly under the table at The Oval too.

I was promoted to the second team, coached by Sammy Ewing, and kept on scoring. The following season, I started where I'd left off, finding the back of the net for Glentoran seconds. The boss, Gibby MacKenzie, even asked me to train with the first-team squad on a couple of occasions. Then it came – the call I'd been waiting for. One September evening as I was jogging around the pitch with Harry Creighton (known throughout the League as 'the Senior Pro'), I was told Gibby wanted to see me in his office. 'You might be getting a chance in the first team,' Harry reckoned. At last, I was going to emulate my father and play in the Irish League. I took a couple of seconds to compose myself, knocked on the manager's door and went in. The boss didn't stand on ceremony, that wasn't his nature. In his clipped Scottish brogue, he informed me that Cliftonville needed a left-winger and Glentoran were letting me go. That, as they say, was that. As I walked away, the tears welled up in my eyes. Gradually, the realisation hit me that Gibby MacKenzie didn't rate me and the Glens didn't want me. To make matters worse, I was being sent to Solitude. The way I was feeling, it was a fitting destination.

What a fall from grace. Well, that's how I felt at least. From The Oval and one of the country's top clubs to Solitude, the League's last bastion of amateurism and home to one of its worst teams. The refusal to pay players made Cliftonville a less-than-attractive proposition to the leading lights of the local game, hence they'd finished bottom of the table for the past seven straight seasons. It did, however, have an upside. As I was about to discover, that Corinthian spirit left little option but to blood young players, in many cases before they were ready. I wouldn't have long to wait for *my* opportunity. Four days after the door closed behind me at The Oval, I was turning the handle on one marked Cliftonville 1st XI. More than ten years had passed since that frail-looking youngster posed in the bedroom mirror wearing Harryville School blue. Now it was the red shirt of Cliftonville that was taking on special significance. As I slipped it over my head, the Irish League debut I'd dreamed about was just minutes away.

Chapter Two

FROM SOLITUDE TO A GLORIOUS SEAVIEW

We won a corner and I sauntered to the edge of the penalty box. Standing directly in front of me looking meaner than a hungry grizzly was Crusaders defender Norman Pavis. Norman and I might as well have been from different planets. He was a veteran of many League campaigns; I was young and inexperienced. He was built like the proverbial brick outhouse; I was thin as a toilet brush. He was the quintessential football hard man, with a fearsome reputation; I was a typical winger, not too fond of the rough stuff. It's not to say that big Norman couldn't play a bit – far from it – but his penchant for kicking lumps out of the opposition encouraged fans the length and breadth of the country to regard him as something of a hate figure. Not so many years before, I had enthusiastically contributed to the chorus of abuse hurled his direction at Ballymena Showgrounds. Now I was within kicking distance.

Facing down a man who enjoys cult status can be a sobering experience when you're only a handful of matches into a senior football career, and Norman had no intention of letting me off lightly. First, he growled out some immensely practical tactical instructions to his goalkeeper: 'Come and get it – fists, knees, everything!' Then, just as I shuffled closer to goal, he barked, 'Where the f*** are you going?' I froze to the spot. Norman waited. I knew this was one of those defining moments. Here, right now, I could lay down my marker, I could stand up for myself and send a clear message to the bully-boys in the Irish League that this Ballymena boy wasn't going to be intimidated. All it required was a single rapier-like thrust of the Fullerton wit. On the other hand, there was no point in being hasty. After all, time was on my side. Surely there would be another opportunity to exact revenge on Norman Pavis for scaring me half to death. And so, the impressive course of action I *actually* executed that day at Seaview was as follows: I stood completely still, the look complemented by startled bunny eyes and a mouth that drooped wide open.

That was your lot at Cliftonville. From day one, it was a learning experience, with my Irish League debut in 1963 somehow managing to be both memorable and instantly forgettable. By that, I mean that I scored the game's opening goal, always a thrill, and never more so than when you're making your first appearance; it's just that the opposition, Ards, followed my strike with seven of their own. Playing with the League's whipping boys, the best I could hope for were those occasional moments of personal triumph (a goal here, a goal there), which were inevitably overtaken by collective failure. Don't get me wrong, I was no shining light held back by those around me. In fact, I was infuriatingly, consistently inconsistent. Mind you, if there was anything positive to be gleaned from getting played off the park by sides virtually every week, it was that at least I was picking up a few handy tips along the way. Even that baptism of fire against Ards brought with it more than just the humbling experience of a

7–1 scoreline. It taught me that hogging possession is one of the cardinal sins.

I liked to have the ball at my feet. The rest – tackling, chasing back – was always a chore by comparison. There's nothing to beat the feeling of beating a defender, a shimmy here, a drop of the shoulder there, leaving him chasing shadows. It was one of my real strengths. It was also one of my weaknesses. I remember the advice offered before that senior debut for Cliftonville. It centred on the fact that, as a ball-player, I would enjoy the pace of the senior game. It was music to my ears that there was less hurly-burly than in the lower leagues, that, in short, I could expect more time on the ball. Unfortunately, I didn't quite appreciate the subtleties. Sure enough, the defence didn't attack mob-handed, but I soon realised that every second I dallied gave their colleagues a chance to cut off the ball's escape route. Every crowd-pleasing jink closed down my options for pass and cross. The key to this wing-play lark was clearly timing, knowing when to beat the man and when to release the ball early. It didn't pay to take people's utterances about time on the ball at face value. I tried to bear that in mind throughout my career, although there were lapses. One, in the European Cup no less, brought with it a painful souvenir.

I take little pride in my move from Cliftonville to Derry City. Sure, it brought me to European football, but it also demonstrated a naked ambition on my part that surprises me to this day. I'd scored at the Brandywell on a couple of occasions, and I'd given Jimmy McGeough (who had played for Sheffield Wednesday) and Jimbo Crossan (younger brother of Northern Ireland international John 'Jobby' Crossan) difficult afternoons. I also knew that Cliftonville was a shop window, so it wasn't a total surprise when another Ballymena man, Derry's left-back Billy Cathcart, confirmed his club's interest. I suppose it would be called 'tapping up' in today's parlance, and I admit to playing my part in the intrigue. Knowing Derry wanted me, I went to see Major Shields at Solitude, told him I was going to work in England and secured my release. A few weeks later, I signed for the Candystripes. It's out-of-character behaviour that has bothered me more in later years than it did at the time. Then, I was just a young man in a hurry.

You just don't think when you're young. Spur-of-the-moment decisions seem to come easy when you're not restricted by the baggage of maturity. How else can you explain my choosing to go on a first Continental holiday, to the Costa Brava, in the same week as Derry City played Oslo in the first leg of a European Cup tie? A starting place was virtually mine for the taking, what with regular left-wing Roy Seddon out through injury. No, off I went with my old mucker Maurice Falls for some sun, sea and sangria in the Pearl of the Costa Brava, Tossa de Mar. Luckily for me, fate was on my side. Derry City overcame the Norwegian side, earning the club a double-header with Belgian champions Anderlecht. And what do you know? Roy Seddon, who had returned for the second leg against Oslo, was sidelined again.

On 26 November 1965, I ran confidently out in front of 25,000 fans in Brussels. The source of my self-assurance was my teammate and former Northern Ireland international Fay Coyle, who, just a few minutes earlier, had passed on his experience of foreign opponents. 'You'll enjoy this,' he said. 'European defenders will stand off you,' he said. 'They'll let you play,' he said. I wish he'd mentioned it to their right-back, George Heylens. One of ten Belgian internationals in the Anderlecht side, he wasn't a big fan of letting anybody play, especially a cocky wee sod from the auld sod. Instead, with only five minutes played, he performed that classic full-back manoeuvre. The pass came to me knee height. I cushioned it with my first touch, but just as it nestled at my feet, dear old George launched himself, studs up, from ten yards. He hit me like an Exocet missile, catapulting me over his shoulder into a crumpled heap. It was just his way of saying, 'Welcome to the match.' As I hobbled off to lick my wounds, I caught Fay Coyle's eye. He shrugged his shoulders and threw me a look that said, 'Well, it's all changed since I was last here.'

For the record, the man who clattered me in such convincing fashion went on to captain his country at the 1966 World Cup finals. Oh, and his club side hammered us 9–0 in an unstoppable display of slick passing and clinical finishing. Maybe it's just as well the return leg never took place. UEFA deemed the Brandywell unfit to host the game, Derry City refused to play it at Windsor Park and neither side would budge. It was my one and only appearance in Europe.

You would think I'd be used to coping with heavy defeats after my sojourn at Solitude, but our humiliating loss in Belgium hurt. Here was I thinking that the Irish Cup win in 1964 and the League championship in 1965 (I joined at the tail-end of that campaign) meant Derry City was a good team. Of course, domestically, we were; it was just that Anderlecht demonstrated that we were merely big fish residing in a very small pond. I think what hit me so hard was the fact that I remembered the Belgians getting thumped over two legs by Manchester United in 1957. They were no Real Madrid, in my eyes at least. Why then were we so outclassed? Where did that leave us?

Thankfully, I didn't have long to philosophise – back in the real world, we were due to face Linfield in the League at Windsor Park on Saturday. It provided an unexpected boost to morale, well, for me at least. The Blues may have beaten us 2–1, but I bagged the game's opening goal, a 20-yard drive past Iam McFaul, who would later play for and manage Newcastle United. As I never tire of reminding Iam every time we meet, that strike was made with my normally redundant right foot. It had been quite a week: my European debut, a goal at Windsor Park and my picture splashed across the front page of *Ireland's Saturday Night*. Of course, all it needed now was a favourable mention in Malcolm Brodie's match report. He was, after all, the man who travelled the globe reporting on World Cups. People respected what Malcolm had to say. I was duly mentioned in dispatches for scoring, but there was one more twist in this week of fluctuating emotions. As I read further, a single sentence brought me back down to earth. It reminded me that I was far from the finished article and that more was expected than the odd goal here and there: 'Derry disappointed overall and apart from his goal Fullerton contributed little else.'

My European adventure was over, but it wasn't the end of my travelling. A few weeks later, I spotted a newspaper advertisement looking for players in South Africa. Now, I don't know if the urge to seek pastures new first sprouted in Brussels or if it was down to my inability to shift Roy Seddon from the first-choice left-wing berth at the Brandywell, but I was soon heading south of the Equator. The wheels were set in motion when I replied to the ad and met up in Belfast with a bloke who had just returned from the country. I learned from him that clubs there offered playing contracts plus part-time work that amounted to a wage of £120 per month. I was ready for a fresh challenge, the hike in salary helped clinch the deal and, despite the obvious distress it caused my mother, I headed for Boksburg, a small mining city about 15 miles from Johannesburg.

This was not a good time in South Africa's history. Only 6 years earlier, 69 demonstrators had lost their lives in the Sharpeville township when police opened fire. Apartheid, in place for nearly two decades, was as deeply entrenched as it was unpopular with the majority black population. The outside world may have been waking up to this rampant racism, as evidenced by boycotts and expulsion from the

Commonwealth, but salvation was a long way off. To put it into context, when I arrived in February 1966, Nelson Mandela still had 24 years of prison life ahead of him. It's different today. We are so much more knowledgeable about the world around us, thanks in no small part to 24-hour-a-day, 7-day-a-week news channels. Back in the '60s, you lived a pocket-sized existence by comparison, encouraging insularity rather than knowledge of the hardships facing the wider human race. That ignorance can be bliss, but it can also mean a rude awakening. The sight of blacks lying dead at the roadside, covered only by a piece of cardboard, or witnessing the degrading way many whites, particularly the Afrikaners, treated the indigenous population was a disturbing dose of reality. But if I was occasionally exposed to the sights and sounds of race hate, most of the time I led a sheltered existence. It didn't escape my attention that Boksburg was an all-white team in an all-white league, but the people around me made it seem the most natural thing in the world. If I knew then what I know now, would I still have gone to South Africa? Probably not. All I can say is that I thoroughly enjoyed the experience but feel guilty about it. At the time, though, I was content just to play my football, work part time as a number-cruncher for British industrial firm GKN (Guest, Keen & Nettelfield), and socialise with expats like Trevor Millar, brother of Ireland and British Lions rugby legend Syd Millar.

I never felt completely comfortable with the social scene in South Africa. There were plenty of enjoyable evenings in Trevor's company, but I missed the familiarity of my mates back home and those nights out at the Flamingo Ballroom. Football was a different matter. From a sporting perspective, there was little not to like about the set-up. The 16-team National League was well organised, the facilities light years ahead of the Irish League, and it provided the opportunity to play against men like Peter Baker, a member of Spurs' great

Double-winning side with Danny Blanchflower. Then there was the travel. I gulped for air on the high veld and then skipped like a springbok when we flew to Durban and Port Elizabeth on the coast. I was 22, fit as a fiddle and flying high. Life, though, was soon to get even better. I was about to meet my dad's idol, Stanley Matthews, not once but twice. The 'Wizard of Dribble' was introduced to the teams before one of our games, that handshake the first fleeting memento. Then, a few days later, Trevor got us tickets to watch the great man play in an exhibition game at the Wanderers Rugby Club in Johannesburg. He had only retired from professional football the previous February, at the tender age of 50. It was a master-class in the South African sun as he bamboozled defenders with feint and dummy. Often they were beaten before his toe touched the ball. The sun also shone on me that day. I won the Wanderers raffle and received a ball signed 'Best wishes, Stanley Matthews'.

Boksburg avoided relegation that season. As a player, I was still blowing hot and cold, but eye-catching goals like the one I scored against Arcadia in Pretoria ensured I was offered a second contract. When I was back home for the summer, the club even sent me the ticket back out to South Africa. I would have gone back, too, but for a girl I'd first met when I was a 16 year old. Linda Russell was her name. I swear that I knew, even then, one day we would get married. I have my pal Brian Blackadder to thank for our first proper introduction. It was no secret to him that I fancied the girl from Kells with the dark, distinctively flicked hair. On the school bus, he told Linda he had a friend who wanted to take her out – Jackie Fullerton. Linda never tires of reminding me that her reply was 'Who's Jackie Fullerton?' We finally hooked up at a dance, and dated a few times before drifting apart. We didn't fall out, it was just that at 17 I was more interested in playing football and having a bit of craic with the lads.

We met again not long after I'd returned from South Africa, only by that time Linda was in a steady relationship. It looked as though my predictions of our marriage were well wide of the mark. Six weeks later, though, some mutual friends engineered a meeting between Linda and me. The chemistry was still there, and not long after, we rekindled our teenage romance. It was not all plain sailing, though. Boksburg wanted me back and were prepared to hold on to my registration if there wasn't a transfer fee. A stand-off ensued. Linda had started a one-year probationary period after qualifying as a teacher from Stranmillis College. Clearly, she was not about to up sticks and swan off to South Africa. I had a choice: stay with Linda and accept that I would be banned from signing for an Irish League club for the term of my contract; or go back and live the bachelor's life in Boksburg. There was no contest.

My New Year's resolution for 1967 was to make the most of the situation. As it was highly unlikely that any Irish League club was going to stump up a few thousand pounds to secure my release from Boksburg and I would be breaking FIFA rules if I signed professional forms for another club without clearance, there was no option but to be patient. Thanks to a friend, Willie Cully, I managed to retain some level of fitness with a few appearances for Bleachers & Dyers of Lambeg in the Amateur League. Then Ballymena man Sammy Hughes, the former star centre-forward with Glentoran, persuaded me to see out what was left of the season with B Division Larne. Eric Adair had cobbled together a great wee team at Inver Park, and, importantly for my rehabilitation from post-South Africa frustration, the dressing-room banter was mighty. You couldn't help but be in a good mood with men like Kenny Wilson around. Win, lose or draw, wee Kenny's repartee rarely failed. After one home defeat, our right-winger Sandor Shiels, Sandy to his mates, was in particularly foul form. The boss had just torn strips off him in the changing-room, singling him out for the hairdryer treatment. As Eric left the room, Sandy slammed his studs on the tiles and said, 'I need to move club!' Quick as a flash, Kenny pipes up, 'From one foot to the other.' Undoubtedly, the highlight of my short stay at Larne was beating Ballymena United at Inver Park in the County Antrim Shield. I was up against former Everton and Scotland full-back Alex Parker and acquitted myself well. It might have been better if that had been one of my off days, for my display started the ball rolling. It would lead me to ignore my better judgement and the advice of my father. It would see me leave Larne and sign for my home-town team.

I would return like the prodigal son, the cheers ringing in my ears as supporters welcomed back one of their own. That's how I saw it, at least. Dad knew different. He'd played for his home-town team and knew the odds were stacked against becoming a prophet in your own land. I'd even seen it myself. Norman Clarke was the player I idolised most growing up. Dubbed 'The Wonder Boy', his left foot was like a magician's wand. A grammar-school boy at the rugby-playing Ballymena Academy, Norman lived all our dreams. Academy's headmaster, Willie Mol, didn't share our appreciation. Rugby was the only sport in his eyes, and it was through gritted teeth that he gave permission for Norman to leave school early one afternoon. The 16 year old had to dash to Ballymena Showgrounds to play against Portadown in an Irish Cup replay, arriving in time to score the only goal of the game, a 25-yard free kick. Now, can you imagine how popular Norman Clarke was with the fans? Well, that didn't stop them turning on him when he dropped below his own high standards. I'd heard them tear strips off him, yet there I was grinning from ear to ear as I scrawled my name on the contract. Did I really believe I could succeed where a genius like Norman had failed? No. It was more that I was desperate to return to senior football

– that and a bit of flattery. I supported Everton as a lad, and now one of their former players wanted me to play for him. Alex Parker just pressed the right buttons.

I doubt very much if the 'How to Win Friends and Influence People' handbook includes a section on flying the coop at your earliest convenience. It's more likely to suggest staying around, winning over any doubters and maybe even scoring a couple of goals. So what did I do a couple of matches into my Ballymena United career? I married Linda (on 15 August 1968) and jetted off on honeymoon to Tossa de Mar, the same resort I'd departed Derry City for just before the European Cup. We had a great time, ate plenty, lay around and soaked up the sun; in fact, all the things designed to take the edge off fitness. When I returned, slightly overweight, Alex put me straight back into the team for a mid-week visit to Windsor Park.

If I was surprised at that, it was nothing to what lay in store as I walked into the dressing-room. Getting ready was a red-haired lad I'd recommended to the club just before leaving. We needed a midfield enforcer and I'd told the manager about Roy Coyle. I'd watched him at close quarters on the two occasions Larne played Ballyclare Comrades, and both times he had made his mark on the game. Roy didn't stay around long with Ballymena before transferring to Glentoran and later Sheffield Wednesday. Suggesting Roy to Alex Parker was one of the few constructive things I did at Ballymena.

Not long after kick-off, my shirt was soaked in sweat. You could almost smell the paella and sangria seeping through my pores. The extra pounds I'd piled on didn't exactly enhance my performance, but I still managed to give Linfield's full-back, Ken Gilliland, a busy evening's work. He was my sort of full-back. Ken let you play; he wasn't the sort to kick you into row Z. Take away the threat of physical pain, and I was your man. It was opponents like Johnny McCurdy I always struggled against. If you regard the wing-back as a modern invention, think again. Coleraine's right-back was a one-man team. He was in perpetual motion, launching as many attacks as he stopped. And when it came to those defensive duties, he was as uncompromising as they come. Only once in my career did I get the better of Johnny, scoring twice and receiving the Man of the Match accolade. It's a measure of the respect I have for the man from Ballymoney that I treasure the memory of that match like a trophy. If I could only have played like that in the sky-blue shirt, things might have been all right. But I knew my performances were mostly below par. In case I was unaware of this, local supporters like George McGarry were there to remind me. George was notorious for getting things off his chest in – how shall I put it? – a forthright manner. If there was any consolation, it was that he'd badmouthed players a lot better than me.

I was struggling, the team was struggling and the stick was getting worse. I went to see Alex Parker and asked for a move. It was Glenavon who came to my rescue. Legendary former Belfast Celtic player Jimmy Jones ended my agony by agreeing an exchange deal with centre-forward Jim Ryles. Who got the better deal? Well, let's just say that I made a competent if not spectacular Glenavon debut against Ards. Big Jim, on the other hand, helped the Ballymena public get over the loss of Jackie Fullerton by bloody well scoring a hat-trick in a 5–0 win. At the beginning of December, just two weeks after I'd left Ballymena, Alex Parker was sacked. A mate of mine met that old terrace wag George McGarry not long after. 'Can you believe it?' he enthused. 'Santa Claus has come early. We've got rid of Fullerton and Parker in the same month.'

Glenavon's results mirrored my own performances over the next three and a half years. There were more good days than bad but we never achieved the reliability that brings silverware. I was happy enough, though. In fact, the thought of moving from Mourneview Park didn't enter my head.

That is, not until January 1970 and a bad tackle by a former teammate from Derry City. In fairness, it wasn't Dougie Wood's normal modus operandi, but he still caught me high and late. There was a nasty crunch as his kneecap connected with the soft tissue on the inside of my knee. The jab of pain suggested all was not well, my inability to stand confirmed it. The ligament damage I suffered that afternoon kept me on the treatment table until the end of the season. I didn't kick a ball for Glenavon again. Early in the summer, Jimmy Jones phoned me to say the Lurgan club was letting me go. That call hurt. Rumours had been circulating for a while that I had been fit to play towards the end of the campaign but had chosen to feign injury and pick up my money. Apart from the fact that you played for the love of the game, not the £6-per-week wage, it was downright insulting. I'd gone to Glentoran's renowned trainer Bobby McGregor in an attempt to speed my recovery, had suffered four weeks of agony as he massaged my tangled ligaments into some semblance of order. Jimmy, though, clearly had reservations about my commitment to the cause. Suddenly, as the receiver clicked on the phone, I had a measure of insight into how Sammy Magee felt just a few months before.

Sammy was a cracking player who had represented the Irish League on numerous occasions against its counterparts in England, Scotland and Wales. He was coming into his prime and was an integral part of our set-up. It was about 45 minutes before the match was due to kick off when it all kicked off, so to speak. Jimmy Jones was chatting to players individually and sidled up beside Sammy just as he was pulling on his shirt. Jimmy, who occasionally lacked something in the man-management department, said he needed more effort. You could see straight away that Sammy was less than overjoyed, and he asked what Jimmy meant by that. 'I need you to be more aggressive in the tackle,' the boss explained;

but he didn't stop there: 'My Aunt Aggie could tackle better than you.' As Aunt Aggie's name reverberated around the changing-room, Sammy calmly took off his shirt, handed it to Jimmy and said, 'I suggest you get your Aunt Aggie to play.' With that, he dressed and walked slowly out the door. A few of the senior players, Errol McNally, Jackie Hughes and Freddie Clark, went after him. They couldn't persuade Sammy to come back that Saturday, or any other for that matter. Not only did he never again pull on the blue shirt of Glenavon, he never played again at all. Sammy Magee was just 27.

I didn't take my departure quite as seriously as Sammy had his. I was upset, yes, but at two years older, I was also conscious of a gradual physical decline. I was busier than ever, working in cost accountancy for STC (Standard Telephones and Cables) in Monkstown, and the balancing act between work, training and playing was increasingly difficult to execute. A decision on retirement had to be taken some time, so why not now?

Given the circumstances of my departure from Mourneview Park, it's ironic that a former Glenavon player should be instrumental in persuading me to give it one more go. Billy Johnston, who was capped twice by Northern Ireland, had only recently taken charge at Crusaders. His career at Oldham Athletic had been cut short by an ankle injury, and he was dipping his toe into the murky waters of management. There was no big budget at Seaview, but Billy had partly inherited and partly recruited a useful-looking blend of youth and experience. There were young guns like Tom Finney, who would go on to play for Luton Town and Northern Ireland, John Flanaghan, Liam Beckett, Bobby McQuillan, Drew Cooke and Lawrie Todd. The more experienced campaigners included John McPolin, an accomplished wing-half despite being only in his mid-20s; Walter McFarland, who had taken over the enforcer's role from Norman Pavis; goalkeeper Jimmy Nicholson; and, eventually, me.

It was B Division side Carrick Rangers who first offered me another season in the game. The lure of senior football and Billy Johnston's leadership convinced me, however, that I should throw in my lot with Crusaders. Funny that some people thought I'd been more interested in money than playing during that lengthy spell on the sidelines, for it was Carrick, despite their junior status, that had offered the best signing-on fee and weekly wage. It proved to be one of my better decisions.

You've got to admire players who step up to the plate week in, week out, especially at clubs like Linfield and Glentoran where the pressure to succeed can be suffocating. I take my hat off to guys like Sammy Pavis, Lindsay McKeown, George Dunlop and Jim Cleary, who were expected to, and did, produce eight or nine good games out of every ten over long careers. I, on the other hand, could survive with a ratio more akin to three good ones out of ten. My Achilles heel was still that inability to perform consistently at my best. However, at Crusaders, for one glorious season, I did just that. The key to it was a good start. A couple of goals in my first two games grabbed the fans' attention; a hat-trick against Glentoran at The Oval in match number three ensured they were well and truly on my side. A 2–1 defeat of Linfield just before Christmas did wonders for our collective self-belief. Only after beating the Blues did we consider ourselves title contenders, and even then we knew it would take a lot more of the same.

It all came down to the last four matches of the season. The destination of the Gibson Cup was in our hands. If we won all four, the trophy – for which Crusaders had been competing since they entered senior football in 1949 – was on its way to Seaview for the first time. There were anxious moments, but as we travelled to Inver Park for the last game of the 1972–73 season, the fate of the title was still in our hands. Larne had been brought into senior football as mid-season substitutes after another of my former haunts, Derry City, withdrew (the burning of a Ballymena United bus by so-called supporters had made the club's position untenable). If this was the title decider for us, it was also a big day for the League's new boys, and it was clear they had no intention of seeing us crowned champions on their patch. The pre-match hype included an inflammatory article by the home side's striker Marty Bell, a picture of Inver Park with a coffin superimposed on it and the headline ' "We'll bury Crues," says Marty'.

If it was intended to psych us out, it didn't work. We were 4–0 up after just 22 minutes. We looked to be home and dry until Larne pulled two goals back early in the second half. Nerves began to jangle, suddenly Inver Park's tight terracing and sloping pitch felt like they were closing in around us. Then a ball came to me just inside the penalty box. I controlled it with my chest and, as it dropped, volleyed it into the far corner. It was all the breathing space we needed.

I'll never forget the sight of grown men crowding around us, tears streaming down their faces. They'd waited a long time for this. As a Ballymena man, I could empathise with the supporters that day. For clubs outside Belfast's 'Big Two' success is something hoped for rather than expected. To have won the title with my home-town team would have been magical, but I'm still immensely proud of what we achieved at Crusaders. On a personal level, I had at last added reliability to my armoury. My tally of twenty goals for the season was just two short of the club's top scorer, Tom Finney, ensuring a summer free from fears of finding myself without a club. Could we cope with Dynamo Bucharest in the European Cup? Could we retain our title? Could I match the previous season's contribution? There was no shortage of motivation to prolong my football career, yet I chose to walk away. A better offer had come along, one I just couldn't refuse. It was a transfer to television that took me totally by surprise and changed my life.

If revenge is indeed a dish best served cold, then no one could accuse me of scrimping on preparation. The chance to settle my account with Norman Pavis, the man who'd made my first senior visit to Seaview so intimidating, came, unexpectedly, 15 years after our penalty-box encounter. Football was now only a pastime, the Ballymena Over-35's League Cup competition the showcase for my eroding talents. I may have been a yard slower, but I still enjoyed the cut and thrust of the game, and the camaraderie in the changing-room.

We'd reached the semi-final, although my former Glenavon teammate Jackie Hughes and myself had picked up hamstring injuries in the process. Desperate to reach the final, our manager Stewarty McAuley took me aside and asked if I could recruit a couple of my football pals from Belfast. I think he truly believed that some sort of ex-players' network existed that could be accessed using a secret code word. I, on the other hand, knew it wasn't going to be easy to find a decent centre-forward and defender at short notice. Then it came to me, two players who would fit the bill nicely, and, what's more, both from the same family. The Pavis brothers provided the perfect solution. Sammy, the former Linfield goal-scoring machine, and Norman, the teak-tough Crusaders half-back. Amazingly, both lads agreed. All that was required now was for the brothers to live up to their billing.

If the Pavis siblings were struggling in any way to prove their pedigree, it didn't show. The team won 4–0, Norman strolling around at the back like Beckenbauer and Sammy scoring all four goals. Just like all those years ago at Seaview, Norman was going to get the better of me. Only, this time, the humiliation would be in my own back yard. I mean, who in their right mind would let Jackie and I (who had declared ourselves fit and available) back into the team? Then it happened. Stewarty only goes and hands me on a silver platter the chance to get one over on big Norman. He drops the Belfast boys and reinstates us. Finally, I could answer that question Norman had bluntly posed all those years ago. If he really wanted to know where I was going, it was to the final, to pick up my winner's medal. It would have been, should have been, the perfect retort. Norman and I joke about it now, but the last laugh's definitely his. For Jackie and I played like a couple of old women and we lost the final 1–0.

Chapter Three

FROM PENALTY BOX
TO GOGGLE-BOX

My stomach was in knots and my mouth so dry I could barely prise my lips apart. I stumbled over one line of script, then another and another. Self-belief shot to pieces, I somehow struggled through to the end of the programme. It had only lasted eight minutes, yet that was more than long enough to illustrate vividly on-screen nerves at their debilitating best – or should that be worst? How could it have all gone so horribly wrong? Only seven days earlier, I had made a relatively assured live television debut fronting the same Saturday results programme, and that had been 25 minutes long. In fact, I was at pains to point out to my producer Derek Murray over dinner that I hadn't been nervous. 'Don't worry, you will be,' he said with a laugh.

Did I listen? Apparently not, for the following Saturday afternoon, just a couple of hours before I was due in studio, I strolled into my former stomping ground Seaview to watch the first half of the Crusaders match. A few 'I saw you on the telly' comments helped massage the old ego and, as I sipped on a brandy and ginger, it was as if I didn't have a care in the world. The absence of opening-night butterflies allied with the fact that this week's programme was considerably shorter had lulled me into a false sense of security. I'd mentally prepared for the possibility of making a fool of myself on the first programme, and that had focused my mind and helped me through. Now I'd taken my eye off the ball. Of course, experience now tells me a concise programme invariably means more crammed in. That's more pressure and less time to recover from any punctured composure. I mistook beginner's luck for rule of thumb and paid the price. But then, I was new to this game and my transition from penalty box to goggle-box had been a swift one.

Down's legendary full-forward Seán O'Neill slotted away his last spot kick to earn bragging rights for the Gaelic football fraternity. In second place and doing his bit for rugby was the mercurial Mike Gibson. I finished third, just about saving face for Irish League footballers. It was December 1972, and Ulster Television's *Sportscast* programme, presented and co-produced by Gordon Burns, had just finished shooting its *Superstars*-style penalty-kick competition. The concept was simple: take four competitors from three sports and, quite literally, put them on the spot. Fate had a hand in my inclusion alongside genuine stars like Messrs O'Neill and Gibson, with the programme's producers deciding to use the current goal-scoring chart as their criterion for selecting the footballers. I was lying fourth, bagging the final place in the Irish League line-up. But how did taking a few penalties help to kick-start my television career? Well, it may have been a three-times All-Ireland winner who grabbed the plaudits on the pitch, but it was me who performed off it.

We had all been invited, after recording, for the customary drinks and nibbles back at Havelock House, headquarters of Ulster Television. UTV's controller, Sydney Perry, was doing the rounds in the green room (television-speak for the hospitality area), shaking hands and chatting briefly with each guest. When my turn came, we really seemed to hit it off. Sydney was a genial Englishman with a particular passion for cricket, and we shared stories and opinions on the game's great bowlers and batsmen. It didn't stop there. Football, rugby and snooker were touched upon in a chitchat lasting considerably longer than the others. Sydney didn't seem to mind that I was monopolising his time, and I had my own theory as to why. Some time before, I had expressed to Robin Walsh, a friend from cricket who also happened to be UTV's news editor, an interest in getting into sports journalism when I finished playing. It was, however, nothing more than a notion. There was certainly no game plan. In fact, the height of my ambition was the chance to pen a few match reports for the local rag, although that clearly hadn't stopped Robin passing on my predilection towards a media career to his boss.

It was January before our paths crossed again, this time at Seaview on the afternoon of our Irish Cup tie with Glentoran. Crusaders may have been riding high in the League and therefore confident of Cup success, but that didn't prevent the Glens knocking us out of the competition by the odd goal in three. That defeat hit us hard, and fully aware that I'd contributed little to our cause, I shuffled off the pitch through the narrow exit. As I headed for the sanctuary of the dressing-room, I suddenly noticed Sydney Perry and Robin Walsh. Robin gave me the thumbs-up and shouted that they'd meet me in the social club after I'd changed. Behind closed doors the mood was not good. Winning is a habit nobody likes to break, particularly not at home and in the Irish Cup. It was more like a morgue than a dressing-room, and, influenced by the prevailing atmosphere, I contemplated heading straight home.

It was only curiosity that stopped me making a very big mistake. I wanted to know why Sydney and Robin were at the game, so, despite my less-than-delightful mood, I stepped through the social-club door. Within seconds, Robin made his excuses and, leaving Sydney and I to talk, disappeared through the swirling cigarette smoke in search of drinks. Conversation was convivial enough, and Sydney asked if I'd enjoyed recording the penalty-kick competition. Then, with no hint of a warning, he got straight to the heart of the matter. 'Jackie, would you be interested in working in television?' Now there's a mood-changer for you. One minute I was feeling like drowning my sorrows with the rest of the team, the next I was trying to contain my delight. Momentarily taken aback, I managed to repeat what I had originally told Robin. Yes, I was interested in sports journalism, but I'd never contemplated television. Sydney just smiled at me and said, 'I think you might have a chance.'

There's nothing quite prepares you for the first time you gaze down the lens of a television camera. It's a one-sided world, with no interaction, no reaction, just this piece of metal and glass staring blankly back at you. There are strategies, though, to counteract this disconcerting coldness. I turned to my family; more specifically, my Aunt Margaret (Lester). Margaret was a great fan of mine who just loved seeing her wee Jackie on the box. So I thought of Auntie Margaret sitting at home when I looked into the lens. I personalised the process, and later added some fine-tuning. When I was working on football, I imagined I was speaking to Tommy Patterson, a pal of mine from Harryville and an ardent Ballymena United supporter. For rugby, it was another friend, Ballymena accountant and oval-ball fanatic Jimmy Stevenson.

Now, tricks of the trade are one thing, but there's really no substitute for natural ability. There's a skill to exuding calmness on camera, or at least giving the impression of serenity. Some never discover the secret to appearing comfortable in what is an uncomfortable position. I'm one of the lucky ones. It didn't happen straight away, mind. My first screen test at UTV, for example, was characterised by a monotone drawl. The delivery, too, was so wooden I had splinters. I reviewed that original audition tape before my second screen test, took on board what Gordon Burns had to say on the subject and resolved to do better.

I actually had a former teammate at Derry City to thank for winning over the select audience that viewed my second stab at studio presenting. Eddie Mahon, a fine goalkeeper and quite a character, was drafted in as a token studio interviewee. We chatted about his career, and I quizzed him about the infamous bus-burning incident at the Brandywell. Derek Murray would later tell me that the fact that I had asked the 'difficult' question had helped seal the deal. It had demonstrated a journalistic edge, apparently; pretty ironic, considering my lack of experience in that area.

No one knew better than me that my CV was devoid of any relevant media training. I was so sure this would eventually lead to my downfall that it prevented me from seeing the wood for the trees. That's why it never crossed my mind that I might actually be auditioning for the position of presenter, as a replacement for the Granada-bound Gordon Burns. The clues were there. Somewhere in my brain there had been a flicker of recognition that the Eddie Mahon studio interview was Gordon's territory, but that was quickly dismissed. I mean, the penny still didn't drop when Sydney offered me the job. The poor man had to spell it out for me.

I suppose you could say I had an eventful start to the summer of '73. First, I became a dad again when our second son, Nicky, was born on 1 June; then, three weeks later, I was called to UTV for a meeting with Sydney and Derek. I listened to their critique of my performance with a mixture of trepidation and expectation. The camera liked me, they said. I had also done well in the studio. Finally, Sydney says, 'We'd like you to join the *Sportscast* team.' The least Mr Perry could have expected after delivering that little line was a smile, maybe even a thank you. Yet I probably looked more puzzled than pleased. To be honest, I didn't really know what joining the team meant. Did they want a runner or someone to make the tea for Gordon Burns? Such were my modest media aspirations that I was just hoping to be one of the match reporters on a Saturday. In the end, my face turning crimson with embarrassment, I had to ask. And what do you know? Just as he had five months earlier in Seaview's social club, the cricket-loving Englishman hit me for six. 'We see you as presenter of the programme,' said Sydney.

I managed to hold myself together long enough to hear that I would be paid £25 per programme, four times what I'd been earning as a footballer. I even succeeded in conducting a half-decent conversation with Derek as I left the building. It was only when I got home that it finally began to sink in. It's no exaggeration to say that my life was transformed on 22 June 1973. I wasn't completely sure *how* it had happened, but a wee lad from Harryville housing estate had somehow walked off the football pitch and straight into television.

For the next three years, I combined working part time at UTV with my accountancy job in Monkstown. The two roles could not have been more contrasting: one was ordered, safe, monotonous; the other, real seat-of-your-pants stuff. Sometimes good, sometimes bad, each *Sportscast* programme added to the credit column. Experience was the key, so I kept my eyes and ears open and tried my best to learn from my mistakes. From day one in the business, there were also plenty of people willing to volunteer their time and expertise. Before leaving for Granada (and later network fame with *The Krypton Factor*), Gordon Burns had selflessly guided me through those cringeworthy screen tests. There was on-screen political correspondent and off-screen sports producer Derek Murray, with his pearls of wisdom. I had experienced colleagues like Leslie Dawes to call upon, and I had ready-made role models available at the touch of a button. Studying the methods of men like Dickie Davies, Frank Bough, Brian Moore and David Coleman helped me develop a style. Davies, in particular, became my idol. I unashamedly modelled myself on the *World of Sport* presenter with the go-faster stripe in his hair, plagiarised his easygoing 'Hi there, good evening and the warmest of welcomes', imitated his idiosyncrasies. Gradually, just as Sydney Perry had told me I would, I developed my own approach. I began to loosen up, to lose that far from flattering presenter-in-a-straitjacket look. There were still clangers, and plenty of them – that's the nature of the business. It's just that as time goes by you learn to handle them better. In the beginning, though, it's like being back at school. In fact, my education in the ways of the television world began the very first time I wielded a microphone in anger.

Maurice Crabbe was a stalwart of Ballymena Rugby Club, a former Ulster wing-forward and a man who had commentated on rugby for the BBC. In short, he was the perfect interviewee. All I had to do was meet him in Belfast at the launch of one of the first mini-rugby schemes, ask a few questions and report back with the tape. My opening gambit was: 'How many youngsters are there here, Maurice? Four to five hundred?' That was followed by: 'The kids here today, where do they come from, all over the province?' Not content with asking the questions, I was also answering them. It's a classic beginner's gaffe. Maurice was kind to me that day, as I recall. An intelligent chap, he found a way to embellish my already-answered questions with some salient facts of his own.

Interviewing is all about the interviewee; in many cases, it requires prompting, nothing more. A couple of seasons ago, I thrust the microphone in front of Portadown manager, and my good friend, Ronnie McFall. He was fuming at the referee's performance that particular afternoon, and the steam was coming out his ears as he started to speak. When he finally came up for air, just one word was needed from me: 'Really?' That was all it took to reignite the touch-paper and send Ronnie off on another rant. 'Less is more', an adage fitting for most interview situations.

Some mistakes can be put down to inexperience. Some defy explanation. Take the day I made a right Charlie of myself at a Suzuki team announcement. It was big news for the local bike fraternity that Charlie Williams had signed for the Works team. With the Japanese manufacturer behind him, he was an even more potent threat to our own two-wheeled star Joey Dunlop. We'd met before, Charlie and I. In fact, I'd got to know him quite well on trips to cover the Isle of Man TT (Tourist Trophy) races. I liked Charlie, even if he did insist on smoking all of my cigarettes. Now, picture the scene. Charlie is standing in front of the camera wearing a spanking-new Suzuki-branded jacket, on his head a Suzuki cap. Over his shoulder is a gleaming new bike in its Suzuki livery and standing around are mechanics and the like, all wearing Suzuki schmutter. What's my opening question? 'Charlie, you've signed a new contract with Honda . . .' You explain it!

All you can do is smile, and I did a lot of that. I smiled through the first reports I ever worked on, two pieces for a summer magazine programme hosted by the charming Roisin Walsh (now Roisin Dunseith and wife of renowned local broadcaster David). I smiled at football matches I was covering, and I smiled in the studio. My smile became my style. Looking back, I'm convinced it helped me gain acceptance. It struck a chord with people choking on a daily diet of bombs and bullets. With tit-for-tat sectarian murder on the streets outside, sport must have seemed like a blessed relief. Maybe sport and a smiling face were just the antidote folk needed.

There's always a danger, though, as your career and profile develop. You can begin to believe the hype, to get carried away with your perceived popularity. Of course it's flattering when people start coming up to you in the street. But it also pays to heed Derek Murray's warning, issued to me during those heady early days when even a sniff of celebrity could result in swollen-head syndrome. 'Wee man,' he said, for he always called me that, 'you remember that of the people watching you, 30 per cent like you, 30 per cent don't and the other 40 per cent couldn't give a damn.' Not quite what I expected to hear, but probably a more accurate assessment than any of us would like to admit.

It's all the attention, you see, it tricks you into thinking everyone's a fan. The truth is that the men and women who bother to ask for an autograph or to have their picture taken with you are just the ones who like you. The punters who think you're a plonker choose, in the main, to steer well clear. It doesn't mean they don't exist, and every now and again one of them emerges from the shadows. I recall a football match I attended at Windsor Park in the early '90s. I had been working on a radio programme at the BBC and arrived at the ground a few minutes after kick-off. As I made my way around the back of the old South Stand towards the press-box, I noticed a gentleman in his mid-60s coming in my direction. He closed to within ten yards and shouted, 'Ah! Jackie Fullerton!' Another terrace wag, I thought, switching into PR overdrive. 'How ya doing?' I said. 'Can you win today?' As he reached me, and with two policemen standing nearby, he spat out the words 'You're a bastard!' and walked on. It still stings when it happens, but it helps keep feet firmly on terra firma. We enjoy being in the public eye; anyone in television who tells you different is lying. It's also the most natural thing in the world to crave popularity and respect. Mind you, you can have too much of the latter.

We went to Ballymena Showgrounds mob-handed. That's the way it was back then in 1977, before 'streamlining' and 'cost effective' entered television vocabulary. There was my producer, a director, a cameraman, a soundman, a lights man, a PA and me. Our task? To cover the story of how Ballymena United were attempting to rise from the ashes following a fire that had destroyed a grandstand and changing-rooms. The district council (who own the ground) and local community had rallied round and, being the local boy, I knew exactly who to interview. First was Eddie Russell, a teenage goal-scorer in Ballymena's 1958 Irish Cup win and now club manager. Next up was Ballymena man and long-serving left-back Sammy McAuley. Finally, there was the bloke who made the club tick, chairman David McKeown.

I knew David well, and despite his reserved nature, I was confident that with me asking the questions he would be fine. It was hardly new to him. In an attempt to bolster my rather bare journalistic portfolio, I had been penning a few lines for the *Ballymena Guardian*. It wasn't rocket science. Invariably, I would just ring David up, get a few quotes and write my article. Then, when we met before the match on a Saturday, I would check he was happy with what I'd cobbled together on his behalf. 'Brilliant,' he'd nearly always say, 'brilliant' being one of David's favourite words. There was one occasion, though, when the chairman confessed that my stories were causing him a few problems back in his native Braid (a rural area just outside Ballymena). He said the local lads had been wondering where David had suddenly learned all those big words.

It was pretty obvious that David was nervous at the prospect of his television debut, so I ran through the questions with him. I then interviewed Eddie and Sammy, sent the cameraman off to get some shots of the ground and went through the questions once more. This time, I also suggested some answers. A third off-camera rehearsal took place before it was time to do it for real.

I opened with: 'David, the fans have really rallied round.'

'They have,' was David's succinct reply.

I tried another tack. 'You were telling me all sorts of tradesmen have helped.'

'They have.' On and on it went, until finally the poor producer's had enough and hollers, 'Cut!'

He took David aside and explained that all we were getting were very short answers from him and very long questions from me. He added, 'We're sick of hearing from Jackie. We want you, as the chairman, to tell us your story about Ballymena United's troubles.' Just then, that bloody ghost-writing came back to haunt me. For David looks at the producer and says, 'Nah! You're all right. Jackie knows what he's talking about.'

If only more of the young people today had a mentor like Derek Murray. Instead, we live in the era of instant celebrity, where reality television can transform every silicone-enhanced babe and chisel-chinned chap into a presenter overnight. It can't make them any good, of course; that requires something more than barefaced cheek and a bottle of fake tan. I suppose if you make a thing *look* easy, as the Des Lynams of this world do, then its understandable that everybody thinks it *is* easy. However, there's a yawning gap between perception and reality. When the red light comes on, it has the potential to destroy anyone taking the short cut to pounds, popularity and a double-page spread in *Hello!*. It takes time, talent and a fair smattering of luck just to get by in television. To really make it, to truly enter the public consciousness, you need a defining moment. It can come from the most unlikely place. Mine was a routine-looking interview seven years into my television career. Before, I was just the bloke who read the sport; after, I was on my way to becoming what you might term a 'household name'. It's all about making an impact, and, boy, did I do that.

They still shout it at football matches: 'What about Giant Haystacks?' I still hear it in the street: 'There's Giant Haystacks!' It wouldn't be a summer holiday in Majorca (where Linda and I have gone for the past 25 years) if some pasty-skinned tourist from back home didn't yell: 'Look out behind you, it's Giant Haystacks!' You could say it's been my cross to bear, but how can I complain?

It was January 1980, and I made my way to the studio for the interview, which was to be prerecorded. From the moment I stepped through the door, I felt intimidated. It was the sheer size of the man that unnerved me. For those of you not familiar with '70s professional wrestling, Giant Haystacks was one of the star attractions, alongside fans' favourite Big Daddy and the mysterious, masked martial artist Kendo Nagasaki. Born Martin Ruane in London (to County Mayo parents) and brought up in Manchester, this hairy behemoth had a personality so spiky you'd cut yourself just looking at him. Standing nearly 7 ft tall and weighing in at nearly 40 st., he looked like Rasputin on steroids. His stomach started somewhere just below his Adam's apple and threatened to burst out of his oversized romper-suit at various points on the way down. You could have fitted me inside that gargantuan girth like a Russian doll.

My remit was simple. Interview Mr Haystacks about the forthcoming wrestling bill in Northern Ireland, then finish with a flourish. That finale consisted of a prearranged manoeuvre whereby this monster of a man would lift me above his head, perform an intricate turn and then throw me to the ground. He was to take care to cushion my fall, as an inch-thick felt mat was the only thing between the hard studio floor and me. That was the plan.

Forget the prearranged wrestling move, I was struggling to conduct the interview. With the enormous difference in height, my arm was cramping as I tried to hold the microphone up to his mouth. The throbbing in my bicep was nothing, though, to what I was about to experience. Chat concluded, Giant Haystacks grabs me by the backside of my trousers and the back of my head, effortlessly raising me to the roof. Then, deviating ever so slightly from our arrangement, the stony-faced grappler body-slams me onto the mat with a sickening thud. Even when I watch it back now, I wince. 'They say this is kidology,' I groaned in the direction of the camera. Then, as I continued to writhe on the floor, I even managed to thank the man who had just dunked me like a basketball. Giant Haystacks walked away without so much as a word of apology.

Amazingly, I didn't break any bones, but I was badly shaken. My recovery, though, was helped by the response when the piece aired that evening. The phone lines were red hot with people wanting to know if 'wee Jackie' was all right. One bloke who called reception told the girl on the other end of the line that, as a ju-jitsu expert, he only knew one way to deal with a bully like that.

'What's that?' she enquired.

'Hit him a good kick in the balls,' he advised with zest.

I've often wondered why dear old Giant Haystacks treated me like a rag doll that day. Maybe he took offence when I asked him if wrestling was staged, but I reckon he must have been asked that a thousand times before. Perhaps he just took an instant dislike to me. If I had to settle on one theory, it would be that it was his way of putting bums on seats at the wrestling bill. He was the ogre, the scary monster everybody loved to hate. I think he decided that day to live up to his bad-boy billing. I do have a lasting memento of the moment that helped launch my television career: it's a nagging pain in my shoulder that recurs every now and then. I suppose, though, that I should really blame Gloria and *Good Evening Ulster* for that discomfort. After all, I was only called in to conduct the interview with the wrestler as a late substitute. The host, Gloria Hunniford, had fortuitously found herself filming elsewhere that day. Come to think of it, that wasn't the only time my association with Gloria managed to get me into serious trouble.

Chapter Four

A BITTERSWEET TASTE OF HUNNI

Roy McCreadie is a graduate of the Simon Cowell school of diplomacy. The tough-tackling midfielder turned Irish League manager has proved himself to be a past master at psyching out opposition managers, players and fans. Big Roy could start a row in a Tibetan monastery. A few seasons ago, I was scheduled to commentate on a game between his then club, Omagh Town, and League leaders Glentoran. Now, there's no great history of rivalry between the sides, yet by the time Roy was finished it had become a genuine grudge match. Using the local press to toss in a metaphorical hand grenade or two, this wily wind-up merchant succeeded in stirring the pot to boiling point. Such was the animosity that some Glentoran fans threatened to boycott the fixture rather than hand over their hard-earned cash at the St Julian's Road turnstiles. As for the visiting supporters who did make the trip to Tyrone, well, they were determined to have their say.

My commentary position was pitch-side and just left of the segregated area for away fans. As kick-off approached, Roy sauntered past. We exchanged pleasantries and arranged to have a natter after the match. It was around that time that the Glens supporters spotted their nemesis, and, with faces pressed against the fencing, they let loose with a vitriolic volley of verbals. As the abuse cascaded from the terraces, Roy turned to me. I felt his gaze but chose to look away. 'You're on your own, big man,' I mumbled to myself. Eventually, the barrage abated. Then, as suddenly as they had stopped, the shouts started up again. Only this time the chanting wasn't directed at Roy.

'Jackie, Jackie, what about Gloria? Jackie, what about Gloria?' I was completely bowled over. Not because I was on the receiving end of some stick from supporters; it was more to do with the subject matter. Over two decades had passed since the rumour first circulated that I was having an extramarital affair with Gloria Hunniford. Looking at the faces firing such invective at me, I couldn't help thinking that most of these people would still have been in nappies when the story first surfaced. Even my soundman Tom Gray, who was crouching near by, remarked afterwards, 'That's from way back, isn't it?' With a match requiring commentary, I decided to ignore the yelling and get on with the job at hand. Still they kept calling out. Finally, I turned, smiled and gave my tormentors the thumbs-up. To tell you the truth, I was half expecting a cheer or at the very least some acknowledgement that I was entering into the spirit of this good-natured banter. Instead, this bloke barks back, 'Aye, you can smile. But you made love to that woman and then you left her and broke her f***ing heart.' Just then, Mr McCreadie glanced in my direction. If anyone could empathise, it had to be Roy. I raised my eyebrows, but he quickly turned away. I was on my own.

Gloria Hunniford and I come from the same working-class stock: industrious and proud people who also instilled a passion for music. Born in the bedroom of a two-up, two-down terraced house in the County Armagh town of Portadown, she was singing and performing with the Mid-Ulster Variety Group at the tender age of nine. Named after her father's favourite actress, silent movie pin-up Gloria Swanson, I suppose you could say young Miss Hunniford was destined for stardom. At 16, Gloria had progressed to appearances on the vibrant dance band scene, and by 18, she was featuring on radio stations in Canada, after taking up an invitation to stay with her Uncle Jim. It all seemed to sit neatly in the section marked 'meteoric rise', yet it would be another decade before Gloria got her big break.

The decision to record the song 'Are You Ready For Love?' helped pave the way. It reached number eight in the local chart, and the novelty of a singing Lisburn housewife soon came to the attention of BBC Northern Ireland. Gloria was impressive during her interview on BBC Radio Ulster, so much so that she was offered a job. Before long, she was the one doing the interviewing. The rest, as they say, is history. There was a ten-year stint working for British Forces Broadcasting alongside Sean Rafferty. More importantly, BBC Northern Ireland handed Gloria her own radio programme.

It was called *A Taste of Hunni*, and with a two-and-a-half-hour slot five days a week, her profile and reputation soared. She polished her craft, laid rightful claim to celebrity and in doing so became a prime target for television executives on the lookout for talent. When Ulster Television decided it was time to revolutionise their traditional teatime news programme, introducing more features and celebrity profiles, there could be only one choice as presenter. It was 1979 when UTV unveiled its new recruit, the same year another Gloria was belting out the dance anthem that has made her the darling of female karaoke singers from Tokyo to Tobermore. As the decade drew to a close, 'I Will Survive' had New York's night owls gyrating under the glitter balls of Studio 54. Back in Belfast, Gloria Hunniford was on her way to becoming the small screen's new shining star, and I was about to become her studio sparring partner – verbal sparring, that is. I never saw it coming, never for a minute imagined that our on-screen rapport would lead to scandal. I was branded an adulterer, but it was my reputation, not my marriage, that nearly didn't survive.

The camera loved Gloria. She exuded warmth and a confidence born of countless hours' broadcasting experience gained on the radio. Many have found the transition from wireless to television too much to handle. Not Gloria. This was a time before a broadcaster's best friend, autocue, when scripts had to be memorised and delivered. I was in awe at the way she made it all look so easy. I wasn't the only one who was impressed – and influenced. Chat-show host Gerry Kelly, then a reporter on the fledgling *Good Evening Ulster*, shared my sense of admiration. We would sit in the studio and watch Gloria work, looking at one another and wondering just how she did it. Of course, it was radio that taught Gloria to talk, to meander off script, to ad lib. The only difference was that now she was looking down a lens. Elton John, Billy Connolly, Bob Geldof, Donny and Marie Osmond, Van Morrison – they all succumbed to the Hunniford charm as the programme went from strength to strength. Young English producer Alan Wright steered the ship, but there was no doubt about just whose programme it was. I found out the hard way.

I have Gloria to thank for securing me the sport slot on *Good Evening Ulster*. On her arrival, it was still occupied by that experienced campaigner Leslie Dawes, but his straight-up-and-down style of broadcasting didn't seem in keeping with the vision of producer or presenter. This was a news programme with a large dollop of light entertainment – right up my street, in fact. It helped me show the public another side to my personality, another dimension beyond the chap who reads the sport. Gloria also played her part to the full, feeding me lines for the quip and the comeback, talking me up as some sort of eye candy for the female viewer. She joked about my wavy hair, introduced me with 'Here he is, ladies', made people sit up and take notice. I was also on five times a week instead of one, and the extra airtime did wonders for my profile. The most important element, though, was the chemistry between Gloria and me. If there's such a thing as professional flirting, then that's what we did. When the red light came on, we switched it on.

Mind you, our warm working relationship didn't extend to taking liberties. I found out to my cost that it didn't pay to get too clever. Gloria had filmed a feature at Belfast Zoo, the piece ending with her kissing a tiger. To avoid coming straight from a shot of Gloria to her in the studio, I was asked to pick up off the back of the story. So I quipped, 'Obviously a tiger with the heart of a lion.' I could hear sniggering from the gallery and from the cameramen on the studio floor. I looked around to Gloria and she was glaring at me. Heading out of the studio, I ran into Leslie Dawes. 'You've done it now,' he said, making it perfectly clear that I'd overstepped the mark. Back in the newsroom, there was the usual facile post-programme chat. Then, through the door stormed Gloria. She pointed her finger at me and said, 'Just you remember whose show this is!' If that didn't put me in my place, our next on-screen encounter certainly did. Gloria made me look like a right girl's blouse. Introducing me, she told the audience that I had been in make-up for four hours, staring at the mirror. She said I'd had my hair in curlers. She stitched me up good and proper. But that's where it ended; there was no bearing of grudges. Gloria had made her point. She'd flexed her muscles, revealing the tough side that would ultimately help her succeed on the mainland. Network radio and television has no place for the weak or meek. Gloria knew that.

My first reaction on hearing rumours that I was having an

affair with Gloria was to laugh. It was a rather nonchalant response that came from knowing it wasn't true. So I treated the gossip as a joke. Others didn't. Image may not be everything in the television business, but, believe me, it counts for plenty. Tarnished reputations can lead to trouble, and I was too naive to see that there didn't actually have to be an affair. The perception was enough. If the man and woman in the street start to believe the rumours, it can lead to an instant and unwanted image makeover. Before you know it, the decent bloke off the box can become the scumbag who's walked out on his wife to shack up with the blonde.

My employers were not quite so slow on the uptake; they knew straight away the potential for damage. They may well also have wondered if it was a case of 'no smoke without fire'. It was perfectly within their rights to ask me what was going on, and that's exactly what they did. I was summoned to Havelock House for a meeting with management. Waiting to confront me was my friend and former producer Derek Murray, accompanied by Jean Clark, a member of the company's middle management. They said rumours were circulating that Gloria Hunniford and I were having an affair. Not only that, apparently I had left Linda and Gloria had parted company with her husband, Don. We were shacked up together in a love nest. The painters and bricklayers had spotted me leaving, and the gardener and plumber had identified Gloria at the same building.

I didn't mean to be flippant, but all I could say was, 'Is it a nice place?'

'Trust you to come up with a funny line,' Derek snapped back. 'This is serious.'

I tried to reassure them. I questioned how it could be serious when I knew it wasn't true, Gloria knew it wasn't true and, more importantly, Linda knew it wasn't true. My conscience was clear. I stressed that I could sleep soundly in my bed at night, but that wasn't enough to put their minds at rest. Derek and Jean asked what I intended doing about the matter. Once more, I appeared to misjudge the mood. 'What do you want me to do?' I replied. 'Go down to the City Hall with a megaphone and announce to everyone that I'm not having an affair with Gloria Hunniford?' Again, it sounded as though I was taking the whole thing lightly, and when Gloria got to hear of my City Hall comment, she accused me of revelling in the notoriety. I wasn't. As far as I was concerned, there was no affair and therefore no point in letting it get under my skin; the best plan of action was to ignore it. It was the classic ostrich approach and a total non-starter. For this was a story that wouldn't stay buried for long.

It was a Friday morning when Terry Smyth, who had taken over from Leslie Dawes as sports editor at UTV, called me into his office. He told me the *Belfast Telegraph* planned to run a story later that day about my affair with Gloria. I knew straight away that I had to speak to Linda. We had discussed the issue previously, but that was unlikely to lessen the shock and hurt when the newspaper came through our letterbox. Of course, contacting my wife was not easy in that pre-mobile phone era. Linda was teaching and I was left with no alternative but to ring the school at lunchtime. I told her about the impending *Telegraph* exposé. It wasn't a pleasant call to make. Linda had always been totally supportive, but it can't have been a bed of roses. Trust is essential to any marriage, but it doesn't make you immune to doubt. My wife and Gloria's husband were the real victims of the rumour mill. The story never did appear, and I'm fairly sure I have Malcolm Brodie to thank for that. I believe that, as sports editor of the *Belfast Telegraph*, he got wind of the article. Malcolm knew both Gloria and me well, I'd discussed the rumours at length with him, and I am sure it was his intervention that led to the story being spiked.

So what ended the whole affair, so to speak? Well, Gloria did. Or, to be more accurate, her soaring career did. In 1981, she was asked to provide holiday cover on Jimmy Young's network radio programme and became the first woman to present a regular weekday programme on BBC Radio 2. The following year, she was given her own Radio 2 show, a seat she occupied for fully 13 years. She went on to become a highly respected national broadcaster, and has won both radio and television Personality of the Year awards. Personality is something Gloria always had in abundance – that and talent. In addition, no one worked harder to achieve success, and no one deserves it more.

We remain good friends. I met up with her at *Children in Need* in 2005. It was the first time I'd seen her since her daughter Caron's death following a long battle with breast cancer. Gloria and I bumped into each other in the corridor of BBC Northern Ireland's Blackstaff Studio. We hugged. She looked sensational, immaculately turned out, as always, and yet there was a strained, pained look in her eyes. 'How are you, darling?' I asked. Her reply was brief: 'Every day's different.' Later that evening, we took part in the entertainment, singing on George Jones's team; it was fun working together again. Don't take this the wrong way – you know how rumours start – but I think Gloria Hunniford is a very special lady.

It was a typical family get-together, a chance for the Fullerton clan to enjoy the craic and catch up on any gossip. The latter clearly interested my second cousin Addy, who appeared anxious for some confirmation of a rumour that had been 'floating around', as he put it.

'Jakey, are yae doing a line wae that aul' thing Hunniford?' he drawled in the local vernacular.

'Do you want the truth, Addy?' I countered with suitable indignation.

'Aye,' said Addy, now sure he was about to hear some sordid details.

'Well, it's not true, there's nothing in it.'

Addy's response, well, it probably explains why I was still getting stick from football supporters in Omagh more than 20 years after the rumour started. I mean, if you can't convince your own family, what hope the general public? For, when confronted with the truth, Addy merely scrunched up his face and said, 'Away tae f***!'

Chapter Five

TAXI FOR MR FULLERTON!

Two taxis pulled up outside the Sidi Saler Hotel in Valencia. I
jumped into the first with Jimmy Nicholl and George Dunlop.
Terry Smyth and Billy Hamilton grabbed the second. All of us
were buzzing. Northern Ireland's 1982 World Cup campaign
in Spain had kicked off with an encouraging scoreless draw
against a decent Yugoslavian side. Now it was time to hit the
town. We had already decided on our destination during
the short flight back from the match in Zaragoza, and it
came as no real surprise that the choice of Suso's, a lively
bar frequented by the Spanish media, met with Billy, Jimmy
and Geordie's complete approval. After all, as members of
the Northern Ireland squad, they had been cooped up in
camp, first for two weeks' training at a university campus in
Brighton, then at the tournament headquarters which was
now swiftly disappearing in our wing mirrors.

   On nights like these, Terry and I were no longer producer
and reporter, the boys no longer international footballers;
we were just friends, out to shoot the breeze and enjoy a
few drinks. Our post-match excursions were a fairly regular

occurrence, and perhaps it was that familiarity that made me take my eye off the ball. For, although this might not have been our first such trip, it was potentially our last. For the boys had forgotten to pass on one fairly important detail. As we sped through the streets of El Cid's former citadel, I was about to discover that Messrs Hamilton, Nicholl and Dunlop didn't actually have permission to leave.

'We're not allowed out. We've sneaked out.' Jimmy Nicholl's disclosure sent my head spinning. All of a sudden, Terry and I had been implicated in a camp break-out. In fact, we'd positively encouraged the contravention of manager Billy Bingham's direct instruction to his players to stay within the hotel's manicured grounds. I hadn't progressed past panic when we pulled up outside the club. As we piled out of the taxis, I pulled Terry to one side and broke the bad news. His reaction, well, it wasn't quite what I was expecting. 'Uh-ohh!' he mocked, a boyish grin spreading across his face. It was the rugby player in him coming to the surface. You know how the oval-ball boys like their clubhouse craic and touring shenanigans. Unfortunately, this wasn't belting out a few bawdy ballads or baring your backside, this was serious stuff. I explained that, if Bingham found out, we would be banished from the team hotel. No access, no stories. No stories, no point in staying. When I'd finished ranting about catching the first flight home in disgrace, Terry was no longer smiling.

Damage limitation was now the name of the game. There was no way our companions were about to turn around and return from whence they'd come, at least not before they'd had a couple of cold ones. Sadly, Suso's, which had seemed the perfect venue prior to Jimmy's revelation, had suddenly become the most unsuitable in all of Spain. For the last thing we needed right now was to get reacquainted with the local press. We'd chatted to some of the hacks over a Suso's lunch not long after arriving in Valencia. They were a decent bunch, but that wouldn't stop them doing their job. Sure enough, it didn't take long for them to realise there was a potential scoop under their noses. We were a couple of drinks into our stay when a snapper sent over some local girls to pose for a picture with Billy and Jimmy. The poor bloke was just about to click the shutter when Terry leapt from his seat like a gazelle, shoved his hand in front of the camera lens and roared, 'No photographs, no photographs!' We didn't stay long after that, although it wasn't the incident with the photographer scaring us off. The truth of the matter is that the players had never intended partying into the wee small hours. For them, this was nothing more than a brief respite from their bubble-like existence. Drunk or sober, though, it didn't really matter to me as we nervously negotiated our way back into the hotel under cover of darkness. I was a worried man.

Terry's timely intervention prevented any incriminating pictures being printed, but not the story. The Spanish press pandered to a public obsessed by anything and everything to do with the host nation and its opponents in Group E, which included Northern Ireland. They were not going to pass up a gilt-edged opportunity like this. A few days after we'd flouted Bingie's rules, just long enough to lull us into thinking we might have got away with it, the excrement well and truly hit the fan. The published piece turned out to be the standard footballers-and-nightclubbing nonsense: big on sensationalism, not so hot on accuracy. For a start, the two players named in the article were Chris Nicholl and John O'Neill, two of the least likely to be mixed up in any nocturnal escapade. It just wasn't their form. Billy Bingham knew that better than anyone. He was also acutely aware of the need to put his own spin on the matter. So the public response came in the form of a total denial of any wrongdoing by any of his players. That and the suggestion it was all part of an orchestrated plan to disrupt the harmony in his squad.

Privately, Bingie had his suspicions. Maybe the Spanish journo had only been half wrong, or half right, when he wrote 'Chris Nicholl'. At Northern Ireland's next training session, he called Jimmy over for a chat.

I heard Billy summon our co-conspirator. As far as I was concerned, the game was up. 'Oh my God!' I said, the words tumbling out of my mouth before I remembered that Sammy McIlroy, Tommy Cassidy and David McCreery were all within earshot. We were taking part in a training drill, each of us positioned at intervals around the perimeter of the centre circle. The idea was to control the ball, take a touch and pass it on. My hands-on involvement in Northern Ireland's World Cup training was – somewhat ironically, considering my predicament – the direct result of a personal invitation from the manager. It had all started in Brighton during the pre-tournament camp. Billy noticed I'd put on a few pounds and suggested I join them for some training. Before I knew it, he was asking me to take part in ten-a-side games. Any time a player picked up a strain or was nursing a knock on the sidelines, Bingie called for a 39-year-old broadcaster from Ballymena to bail them out.

Of course, I loved every minute of it. I could still perform the basics with a fair degree of dexterity, and, despite Billy's concerns about my middle-age spread, I was in reasonable shape. By the end of the fortnight, it was all too easy to forget I was only there to make up the numbers, that Roy of the Rovers had more chance of playing in the tournament than I did. On a good day, you could even convince yourself that, if only you were a few years younger, it would be possible to cut it at this level. I didn't want my fantasy football to end, and, thanks to Billy, it didn't have to. He continued to allow me to sweat off some of that 'lard', as he called it, in sunny Spain.

Sammy was the first to ask what was going on. Then Tommy and Dee joined the inquisition. Some of the players were oblivious to any story, others had taken as read the truth of Billy's suggestion it had been fabricated. Not surprisingly, they were anxious to learn more. Gradually, our once-spacious drill area shrank as the others closed in to hear my whispered confession. Soon we looked like a group of old dears doing the hokey-cokey at a church formal. The perspiration dripped off my nose as I tried to hold it together. Jimmy, on the other hand, was dealing with the drama in an altogether more nonchalant manner. Faced with a manager who clearly had the scent of a conspiracy in his nostrils, he chose the only path open to him. He lied. Billy Bingham made it abundantly clear he didn't believe the published names. There was no way it was Chris Nicholl; could it possibly have been a J. Nicholl, though? The boss even tried to prick Jimmy's conscience, telling him that they'd been together a long time, that he was one of his top players. Then he asked the question that begged to be asked: 'Were you there?' Without flinching, Jimmy replied: 'Billy, you know me. I wasn't there.'

Now, I'm not saying we were scared or anything, but when Jimmy rejoined his fellow escapee Billy Hamilton, the big man's suntanned face had already turned a pasty shade of grey. I wasn't doing much better. Nic may have been able to remain cool under pressure, but my clammy countenance had guilt written all over it. Who would be next for interrogation? We waited for the call, trying all the while to pass the ball with the air of innocent men. The minutes ticked past and training carried on without further interruption. When the session finally came to a close, I could see the relief etched across Jimmy and Billy's features. For me, though, the torment was only just beginning. I'd deceived a man who'd taken me into his confidence. Before long, I would have no option but to do it again.

I was leading a sort of double life, like something out of a Marvel comic. You know the type of thing: 'By day he's a professional broadcast journalist, by night he's Squad Conscript Man.' I'd managed to juggle the two fairly successfully up to now, but that soirée in Suso's had upset the equilibrium. I could hide from reality on a training pitch for only so long. At some point, though, I would have to wear my reporter's hat again. I would have to interview the manager for UTV and ask about the nightclub allegations. The following day, our crew set up close to one of the training pitch goalmouths. In my line of vision, just over Billy's shoulder, stood my producer Terry Smyth and our production assistant Anne Young. I did my best to avoid the real issue for as long as possible, asking routine questions about fitness and the form of players. Nagging away throughout the interview, though, was the thought that back at Havelock House in Belfast they would be interested in one thing and one thing only.

Finally, I said, 'Billy, there's a lot of speculation in the Spanish press that some of your players were drinking in nightclubs. What do you know about this?' At this point, poor Anne nearly falls off the wall she's sitting on, Terry's rooted to the spot with his mouth hanging open and I'm just thanking my lucky stars that a suntan masks that embarrassing rush of blood to the face known as 'a beamer'. Billy fielded the enquiry by parading out the Spanish-propaganda line, and we went our separate ways. I felt relieved but also disgusted with myself.

Over the past two decades and more, I've frequently thought about coming clean to Billy. On the occasions we've met up, it has often been on the tip of my tongue. I never quite managed to spill the beans, though. I suppose it was the fear that he would think less of me. Billy was fairly certain something had gone on; otherwise, why would he have spoken to Jimmy Nicholl? But I don't think he ever knew the whole story, until now.

I don't wish to portray Billy Bingham as a killjoy, or, for

that matter, a man easily fooled. He was neither. Certainly, anyone who's ever tried to haggle with Bingie over money will know he's far from a willing dupe. Even my partner in crime at Suso's, Terry Smyth, no mean negotiator himself, met his match when he tried bartering with Billy. The evening they traded blows, metaphorically speaking, was the night of San Jose Earthquakes' visit to Windsor Park for a friendly with Linfield in 1981. It was prior to Northern Ireland's departure for those World Cup finals in Spain, and all eyes were on one man. It was the talk of the country that stateside-based George Best might be brought back from the international wilderness, that the prodigal son might finally get the chance to parade his skills on the world stage. Mr Bingham was to attend the game, run his eye over George and then announce his squad for a qualifier after the final whistle.

I introduced Billy to Terry in the foyer of Windsor Park. The three of us then slipped into a side room to discuss the schedule of events – that and the question of Billy's payment. Earlier in the day, Terry had accused me of shovelling out money hand over fist. He regarded Billy's £100 per interview as extortionate and suggested that my judgement was clouded by my liking for the man. He would address the issue when we met. Terry began in businesslike fashion, explaining to Billy where we would rendezvous for the post-match squad announcement and how I would make my way down from the commentary position (UTV weren't broadcasting the match, but using it as a dry run for their new Outside Broadcast Unit). He ended by telling Billy that for the interview he would be paid £40. There was a pause. Bingie threw Terry a puzzled look and then glanced over at me. I shuffled uncomfortably and stared at the floor. It was as if it had taken time to compute, but Billy eventually found a suitable reply. 'I wouldn't do radio for that,' he said. With each party clearly placing a different value on Billy's broadcasting skills, they agreed to disagree.

Terry asked Billy to reconsider his position and told him that he too would give the matter some thought. They could reconvene to discuss money matters when we got together again after the game.

At the final whistle I made my way down from the gantry to the interview position at the halfway line. Billy was already sitting in the dugout waiting for me.

'George Best's not in the squad,' Terry whispered in my ear.

I took a couple of steps, then turned and asked, 'By the way, how much are we paying him [Billy]?'

Terry says, 'A hundred!'

'You certainly told him,' I fired back.

'But he's very nice, isn't he?' was all Terry could muster by way of defence.

After all, he had just become the latest, but definitely not the last, victim of the Bingham charm.

The evening's other victim, although of another Bingham trait, was, of course, George Best. No one deserved more than George to have his talents showcased at the highest level, but Billy's self-belief enabled him to fly in the face of public support for that happy ending. It wasn't an easy decision. There was evidence to suggest that George could still have made a contribution on the pitch, though he was most definitely past his best. I suspect that in the end his non-inclusion was also influenced by what would inevitably have taken place off the pitch. George's presence in Spain would have led to a media circus, an unwanted distraction from the job at hand. Maybe, deep down, Billy was also concerned that Bestie might just hog all the limelight, leaving none for him and his other players.

Billy Bingham's ability to spot where a good deal could be had eventually earned him the nickname 'Billy FIFA' (as in 'a fee for this, and a fee for that'). To be honest, there was some justification for the moniker. Albeit his good business sense enabled him to bolster the Bingham bank balance, his main motivation was clearly the game itself. He did enjoy making a good deal, though; the ducking and diving really seemed to get his juices flowing. A formidable negotiator, he fought his corner with television companies, adopting a policy of divide and conquer. Billy did separate deals with local radio and television, then with the networks. He even had the confidence in his squad, and the foresight, to put in place a rising scale of fees for interviews with national television should he successfully steer Northern Ireland into the quarter-finals in Spain. There was always an angle to exploit as far as Bingie was concerned. I recall some 'shady' dealings in Brighton pre-tournament, literally. I noticed, on arriving in Brighton, that all the players appeared to be wearing identical sunglasses. Noel Brotherston informed me that the boss had done some sort of deal. He even gave me his shades as a souvenir.

There's no doubt that William Laurie Bingham, a former apprentice at the Harland and Wolff shipyard, was determined to escape the working-class struggles that beset so many of his peers. Brought up in Bloomfield, a few streets away from Danny and Jackie Blanchflower, he strived for financial security in a way people born into money can never understand. I recall Billy's second wife, Rebecca, arriving in floods of tears at our hotel room during the 1986 World Cup in Mexico. She was upset because her husband was planning to take up a lucrative, tax-free club-management job in Saudi Arabia. Rebecca didn't want to go. She pleaded with Terry and me to talk him out of going. 'There's plenty of money,' she sobbed, a reference, I assumed, to money on her side of the family. Fiercely independent, though, Billy wanted to make his own way in life and to make his own money. Really, he just wanted to do his best by his family. Rebecca came round to the idea, and when the World Cup finished, he did indeed desert our shores for a successful two-year spell in the desert.

Money mattered, yes, but Billy was no cash-crazy, cold-hearted disciplinarian. Sure, some of the players were irritated at times that he also feathered his own nest, perhaps envying his business sense, but never to the point where they lost respect for him. As far as they were concerned, it was unimportant in comparison with the positive things the manager brought to the table, not least the extraordinary team spirit he created throughout his time in charge. He made them believe in their individual talents and collective ability. In creating this united front, and exercising a tactical acumen that shouldn't be underestimated, Billy transformed Northern Ireland into a genuine force to be reckoned with. As a player, he had been an integral part of Northern Ireland's first World Cup finals adventure in Sweden in 1958. He witnessed first-hand what could be achieved when a group of footballers are galvanised by a common goal. Billy and his teammates would have walked over hot coals for their manager, the great Peter Doherty. Twenty-four years later, Bingham could demand of *his* boys just about anything.

Man-management is often about treating the players as men, as Billy did in Albuquerque, New Mexico, the choice for Northern Ireland's training camp ahead of those '86 World Cup finals. Each evening, Billy and Rebecca enjoyed a nightcap at the same window seat in the Hilton Hotel. It was a quiet spot that also happened to provide a perfect view of the bar on the other side of the tree-lined avenue. Night after night, Billy watched as Billy Hamilton and Jimmy Nicholl skipped surreptitiously across the street for a little end-of-day drinkie of their own. He never mentioned it until just before our final match of the tournament, against Brazil. 'By the way, boys,' Billy said, 'when we were in Albuquerque, did you enjoy your wee drink every night?' He knew it was innocent enough, that there was little to be gained by making a big deal of it. It was just a matter of eventually letting them know he knew. It was a policy he also adopted with me.

Mexico, with its debilitating heat and humidity, was hard work for the players, and for us reporters. When you've been filming all day, standing around under the intense glare of the South American sun, and then rushing around in taxis to cut and feed material, it's draining. A night on the tiles was the last thing on your mind, and Elton Welsby (ITV's commentator) and I settled into a relaxing routine. We would meet for an early evening meal, followed by a couple of vodka and Diet Cokes. Our duo then became a quartet as Pat Jennings and Gerry Armstrong joined us for a chat and, in their case, a soft drink. It didn't take long before Pat and Gerry made a minor adjustment to the arrangement. Soon we were swapping drinks, a development that made me more than a little uneasy.

'Don't worry about Bingie,' Pat joked, 'he needs me.'

I wasn't reassured. 'Yes, Pat, but he doesn't need me,' I replied.

Billy was aware of the friendship and had clearly noticed our nightly tête-à-tête. On one occasion, I was walking around the hotel swimming pool en route to Pat and Gerry's room. We had arranged to meet and listen to some cassettes. As luck would have it, the glass I was carrying so carefully was filled not with vodka and Diet Coke but exclusively with the latter. Billy appeared from nowhere and asked where I was going. I relayed the listening-to-music line. Next, he asks what I'm drinking. So I say 'Diet Coke' and offer him the glass. There was me thinking Billy trusted me, but he only goes and takes a sip. He knew exactly what had been going on.

Billy seemed to have an innate sense of when it was time to clamp down, and equally of when the boys should be allowed to let their hair down. Deciding to permit a party on the evening of 25 June 1982 was not one of the greatest challenges to that instinct. When you beat the host nation, top your group and reach the World Cup quarter-finals, a bit of a shindig is pretty much a given. And what a party it was. Martin O'Neill said it was as if the whole of Northern Ireland was back at the team hotel, no mean feat as the Sidi Saler Hotel was a good 25 minutes out of the city centre. Many of the players watched the sunrise from up on the balcony of their rooms, basking in the glow of a truly remarkable achievement.

The still of the morning contrasted dramatically with the incendiary atmosphere that had greeted them when they walked out onto the pitch in the Luis Casanova Stadium the previous evening. The noise was quite incredible but not surprising, given Valencia's traditions. Each year at festival time, the local inhabitants gather in the square to watch fireworks – at two o'clock in the afternoon! Your average Valencian couldn't give a peseta for the sight of a Catherine wheel lighting up the night sky; they prefer noise and lots of it. The fiesta actually involves teams vying with one another not to illuminate the heavens but merely to create the most mindless din imaginable. Even Billy Bingham, who would be the most positive thinker at a positive-thinking convention, was gripped by apprehension. 'We were like bulls to the slaughter,' I think is how he described the atmosphere as his players lined up for the national anthems. Hell, no one even thought we'd qualify for the World Cup finals, let alone the last eight. In fact, our form going into the tournament suggested a large helping of ignominy rather than the glory that resulted.

Billy Bingham once lectured me over dinner in Belfast's Europa Hotel. He told me, in that wonderfully Anglicised accent, 'Jeekie, you're good at your job, but you're too nice.' He said I needed to 'ruffle a few feathers' during my interviews. I agreed that it was a weakness in my broadcasting armoury and that it wasn't in my nature to be confrontational. Six months later, I'm interviewing Billy for ITV's World Cup preview. Northern Ireland were on an unenviable run that included a 4–0 defeat to France in Paris and a 3–0 loss to Wales at Wrexham's Racecourse Ground. Keen to impress my network colleagues, and in particular the show's presenter, Brian Moore, I decided to give the feather-tousling a lash. I reminded Billy of the disastrous results against the French and Welsh and asked if he was worried that we could be an embarrassment in Spain. The wee man was livid.

When the camera stopped rolling, he said, 'Jeekie, you were a bit rough there.'

So I played him at his own game: 'Yes, Billy, once upon a time a Northern Ireland manager told me I should ruffle a few feathers.'

He smiled at me through gritted teeth and a pained expression. Just at that moment, the soundman of our English television crew piped up: 'Has anybody told you guys you're like doubles? You're very alike.'

Billy, still seething from what he saw as my Gestapo-like line of questioning, turns to the bloke and barks, 'We've heard it before, now piss off!'

He was right, we had.

Chapter Six

BILLY'S DOPPELGÄNGER

What do a former actor, a Turkish bar owner, a national-television cameraman, and a few dozen Spanish and Mexican reporters have in common? The answer is that they've all bought into the Billy Bingham doppelgänger theory. It all started back in 1980, when the recently appointed manager of Northern Ireland made his way to Ulster Television's Havelock House studios for an interview. It was Bingie's second spell in charge of his country, although the first had apparently gone unnoticed. For, not long after Billy had left the building, Charles Witherspoon, actor and presenter of UTV's *Police Six* programme, called me over to ask the identity of my interviewee. I told him it was the new national football team manager, to which he replied, 'That's you in thirty years' time.' I only had to wait five.

March is usually a very pleasant time of year in Majorca. In 1985, though, I almost found it too hot to handle. We were in Palma for a friendly with the Spanish, and I was about to become the centre of attention. It was the last training session before the match: a light workout for the players, a stern test for me. With no warning, I was suddenly besieged by a mob of local reporters, unrelenting in their pursuit of the Northern Ireland line-up. My attempts at explaining that I was not, in fact, Mr Billy Bingham appeared to be falling on deaf ears, until my mate Andres came to the rescue. The owner of a beach bar I frequented on my family holidays, he repeated my denials in the native tongue. Andres's appeal did the trick that time, but the same thing happened again later that year in Turkey.

It was the night before our World Cup qualifier, and I was strolling along the streets of Izmir with pressmen Malcolm Brodie, Gordon Hanna and John Laverty. We were trying, fairly unsuccessfully, to convince a doorman to let us into a bar when the owner suddenly yells at me, 'Ah, football, Bingham, *Irlande*!' I was just about to put him straight when I felt a tug at my arm. It was Malcolm, who then proceeds to confirm that I am the esteemed Mr Bingham, coach of the Northern Ireland football team. Our excited Turkish friend asked me to predict the score, adding for good measure that he thought it would be 1–0 to Turkey. I diplomatically signalled with my fingers a 0–0 draw.

The next thing we knew, he was welcoming us not just into the bar but into the bosom of his family. Fruit was brought to our table, and the man's wife and her friends joined our company. All appeared to be delighted to have such august company in their humble establishment. We didn't think it was too bad, either. In fact, Malcolm bellows from the other end of the table, 'Jackie! You couldn't beat this!' I throw him a withering look, and, at the same time, the owner's wife leans over and asks why he's just called me Jackie. Caught on the hop, I contrived some cock-and-bull story about my real name being William Jack Bingham and only my best friends calling me Jackie. I looked back at Malky, who shrugged his shoulders in a gesture of contrition. Our host that evening no doubt speaks proudly of the night he had a famous football manager in his bar. Not only that but also the fact that this same manager had the power of prophecy. For, the next evening at the Ataturk Stadium, we played out, as I predicted, a scoreless draw.

I don't suppose the whole lookalike thing bothered Billy that much. He even asked me to impersonate him one evening when I was having dinner with him and Rebecca. Mrs Bingham started the ball rolling by asking me to mimic Bill, as she always called him. Then the man himself chimed in: 'Go on, Jeekie, I know you do it, so just do it!' There followed a brief but excruciatingly embarrassing impersonation.

Billy may indeed have snapped the head off that ITV soundman after he dared to suggest we looked like long-lost brothers, but I can assure the poor chap it was nothing personal. He just got Bingie on a bad day. Like most of us, Billy can be sensitive to criticism, and perhaps it was in the back of his mind too that there was considerable potential for embarrassment in Spain. I mean, you would never call his strategy for success conservative. Against Yugoslavia, in that opening match, he gave an international debut to teenager Norman Whiteside.

At 17 years and 41 days, he usurped Pelé as the youngest-ever player in the World Cup finals. It was David Cairns who first made me aware of Norman. My old Boys' Brigade mate, by then heavily involved with the Northern Ireland Schoolboys set-up, recommended I take a look at this strong and skilful skinhead who was earning rave reviews. Big Norm's monosyllabic post-match interview was not a classic, but, a year later, following his move to Manchester United, we met again. I couldn't believe the transformation. The lad had clearly been learning, on and off the field. For Theo Walcott, see Norman Whiteside. Big Norman arrived in Spain on the back of just one full game for United and twelve minutes as a substitute. However, any fears about the wisdom of Bingham's decision were soon allayed. With his first touch, he shimmied past an opponent, and I thought to myself, 'This lad can play.' A few minutes later, the Yugoslavs attempted to intimidate him with a few heavy tackles. So what does Norman do? He stamps on his tackler's leg. Young he may have been, but no one took liberties with Norman Whiteside.

Billy once told me that he knew as far back as Brighton that this prodigiously talented teenager was going to be a fundamental part of his World Cup plans. It was during one of the practice games. Norman burst through on goal about 20 yards out and, with only big Pat Jennings to beat, he curled the ball into the top corner. Pat looked at Billy on the sidelines. Billy looked at Pat. Neither spoke; they didn't need to. What a player Norman Whiteside turned out to be, for club and country. What a travesty that his career was cut short by injury.

The big Shankill lad was a revelation in Spain, but even he was eclipsed by a bigger bloke from the Falls. Gerry Armstrong was nothing short of astonishing. He has, of course, become synonymous with *that* goal against Spain, but it shouldn't be allowed to overshadow his overall contribution to the cause. Gerry was a bit like a freak of nature, suddenly galvanised into action when the heat of the sun hit his back. Boy, could that man run. At training in Brighton, he made light of what was one of the hottest summers in England for years. In Spain, he just carried on where he had left off in Sussex. Even when he was four years older, he was still capable of leaving his teammates in the shade. When Billy was looking to acclimatise his players at altitude in Albuquerque, he used big Gerry as his barometer of how far to push. I was aware from my playing days in South Africa of the debilitating effects of altitude, the burning sensation as your lungs gasp for a whiff of air. But here was Gerry careering up Bingie's 5,000-feet-above-sea-level mountain-trek course as if jet-propelled. Much to the consternation of his colleagues, who would have preferred a more modest pace, Gerry was one of that rare breed of footballers who just love to train. If his power-packed running infuriated his teammates, it absolutely bloody terrified the opposition defences. In '82, Gerry bagged his first goal in the 1–1 draw with Honduras and then succeeded in making a second, ultimately life-changing, strike against Spain. He added a third in the defeat to France, and within two years was playing in La Liga for Majorca.

I was holidaying on the island when he arrived with his wife and children, a fortuitous development for my employer. Ulster Television looked as though they had really been on the ball, sending their man out to get the scoop, when my interview hit the screens back home. Gerry settled into an apartment just up the road from the one we'd booked for our hols, and, over the next few years, we became even firmer friends. Barbecues at Gerry's were always entertaining, and, whether we were poolside, at Majorca's training ground or down at one of Palma's stylish harbour-front bars, the big man's circle of friends was guaranteed to contain a few familiar faces. I met Mark Hughes during his spell with Barcelona and enjoyed a great night in the company of Pat Crerand (like myself, a Majorca devotee) and Terry Venables, then manager at the Nou Camp. To Gerry's great credit, he proved every bit as successful in Spain off the sward as he was on it – a direct result of his decision to embrace the local lingo. He quickly became fluent in Spanish, a string to his bow that helped secure a slot with Sky Sports. These days, Gerry is a widely respected television analyst of the top flight of Spanish football he graced as a player.

The 1982 World Cup was good to Gerry Armstrong, but then he was one of its genuine stars. It's a fact he was able to confirm for himself, with a quick call home. Martin O'Neill often recounts how his teammate left the hotel to use a phone box just down the street. When he returned, some of the lads casually asked what the craic was back in Northern Ireland. With complete sincerity, Gerry replied, 'They're saying there's only three players at the tournament. Falcao, Socrates and me.' Martin actually repeated the same story recently as part of a speech, only he accidentally included in the tournament's top three an Argentinian. It still got a laugh, of course, but the error didn't go completely unnoticed. Big Gerry just happened to be at the same function and was quick to point out to his former teammate afterwards that it had in fact been Socrates, not Maradona.

The east coast city of Valencia will forever be associated with Gerry and his goal. I returned there in 2002 when we played the Spanish in an international friendly. For good luck, we booked into the same charming Sidi Saler Hotel, and I rekindled my love affair with the Luis Casanova Stadium by starting my *BBC Newsline* report in the goalmouth where Gerry had scored. Everywhere felt familiar, everything felt comfortable, just as it had back in '82. For all of us, Valencia had been quite literally a breath of fresh air.

Madrid, though, was an altogether different proposition. We were forced to up sticks and move to the capital for the second phase. I don't think we ever really settled. Unlike on the east coast, there was no relieving sea breeze, just Madrid's frantic traffic and suffocating humidity. We started the second phase well enough, Billy Hamilton putting us one up against Austria. Unfortunately, that was as good as it got. Despite having the demeanour of a team completely lacking in ambition, the Austrians scored twice, and Billy's late equaliser wasn't enough to prevent them taking a share of the spoils they barely deserved. Up next was France, the same nation that ended our dream at the quarter-final stage in Sweden 24 years earlier. Martin O'Neill did have the ball in the net first, his goal wrongly ruled out for offside. Could we have held on again, just as we had against Spain? I don't know. What I do know is that Platini, Giresse, Tigana and co. were a class act. But for Harald Schumacher's X-rated assault on Patrick Battiston (who was a member of the great Bordeaux side of the '80s) in the semi-finals, they might even have gone on to win the tournament. Certainly, they were too good for us on the day; Gerry's goal only came after the French had scored four. The World Cup adventure was over.

I arrived back in Belfast to be met by Linda and the boys. It was good to be home – at least, it was for those first few minutes. Once we were outside the airport, Linda broke the news that my Aunt May had lost her battle with cancer. The missus then inadvertently let slip that my commentary on the French match had not exactly gone down a storm back home. In fact, UTV's phone line had been red hot, with more than 200 complaints. Apparently, my downbeat commentary had misjudged the upbeat mood back home. Could I really have called it so wrong? I just couldn't let it lie. Over the next few days, I continued to mull the matter over in my head, contemplating what I had done wrong. I was being charged with failing to back Billy and the boys. The accusation hurt; that's why the good-natured stick I received on Saturday afternoon at Solitude stung more than it probably should have. I was still tormenting myself about it when I arrived back in Ballymena. Linda and I had invited our good friends Don Stirling and his partner Marlinda over for a meal, but I was too distracted to play the host.

Finally, I had to do something. I made my apologies to our guests, jumped back in the car and drove to Ulster Television. Closing the edit-suite door behind me, I settled down to watch a tape of the match. I can say, hand on heart, that from my first international commentary alongside Derek Dougan (Northern Ireland versus the Republic of Ireland, 1978) to the most recent, I have always tried to call it as I see it. Sure, a bit of jingoism has to creep into it every now and again, but, if you become totally myopic, you lose sight of the truth. The press asked Billy Bingham about my commentary and he suggested that maybe Jeekie had an off day. My performance was also discussed at management level in UTV.

Well, I stand by my work that day in Madrid's Vicente Calderón Stadium. In my summation at the final whistle, I thanked the team for the wonderful journey, paid tribute to the performances of the players and to the fantastic fans, and name-checked everyone from Bertie Peacock, who spied on the opposition for Bingie, to kit man Derek McKinley. Of course, I did stop short of saying, 'We woz robbed.' You see, I value my integrity. Did Northern Ireland deserve to beat France, or come close to it? No. And if I'd said any different, I'd have been talking absolute cobblers. Maybe, though, I was being too realistic at a time when most folk in their living-rooms were in hysterics. At least someone found my work amusing. My UTV colleague Gerry Kelly never tired of reminding me: 'Oh yes, that's the commentary where you said Northern Ireland didn't have a chance when it was only the pre-match kick-in.'

If Gerry Armstrong was the star of '82, there's no doubt that the main man in '86 was Pat Jennings. The big Newry custodian brought to a close a memorable career, taking in 22 years and a then world-record 119 caps, with a classic display against Brazil. But it wasn't just his performances in Mexico, at the grand old age of 41, that caught the eye. But for his brilliance during the qualifying campaign, Northern Ireland would never have set foot in South America.

The turning point in terms of qualification was 16 October 1985 in Bucharest. We'd done well to beat the Romanians 3–2 in Belfast the previous year, but on their patch the Eastern Europeans were an altogether different proposition.

They were unbeaten at home for seven years, and in teenager Gheorghe Hagi they had one of the world's most promising young players. It was my first glimpse of the man with the wonderfully deft left foot who would be dubbed the 'Maradona of the Carpathians'. Early in the match, it was our own young star Norman Whiteside who broke through on goal. The Manchester United player was at the height of his powers, and you would have bet the house on him putting us in front. When his shot cannoned back off the legs of the Romanian goalkeeper, there was a sense that this wasn't going to be our night. We were wrong. It was like a scene from the movie *Escape to Victory*, with the stadium perimeter lined with soldiers and the raucous home crowd baying for a goal. A goal did come, but, to the disappointment of the 40,000 Romanian fans inside the August 23 Stadium, it was Jimmy Quinn who scored it. From that point on, it became a trademark Northern Ireland backs-to-the-wall battle, with big Pat making a string of great saves and the ever-reliable Jimmy Nicholl clearing two off the line. Boy, did we party that night, and into the early hours of the morning too, as I recall. We all knew the significance of the win, that reaching consecutive World Cup finals was now within our grasp. All we needed was a point against England at Wembley in the final group match.

I was exhausted when we finally called time on the celebrations, but I still had the presence of mind to pack my bags and lay out my clothes in readiness for what would be an early start. The bus to the airport left on time the following morning. Unfortunately, I wasn't on it. I'd fallen asleep again after my early morning alarm call, eventually waking with a jolt. It didn't take long for my worst fears to be realised. Not only was I on my own but the previous evening's revelry had also left me with insufficient local currency to pay my hotel-room extras. At reception, they refused point-blank to take a Western cheque. Suddenly, from over my shoulder, a voice said, 'Mr Fullerton, perhaps we could go to the airport and your colleagues could give you the money?' Great idea, I thought, looking around for my bag. 'It's already in the car,' my sinister-looking companion informed me. This was the era of the brutal Ceausescu regime, and here I was accepting a lift from the secret police. I had little choice, though, so I placed myself completely at the mercy of two blokes with dark suits and demeanours to match. Thankfully, the Romanian secret police were happy to see the back of me. They wasted little time in dropping me at the airport, where I borrowed the £60 from Pat Jennings. Only when my seatbelt clicked into place and the stewardess began her safety routine could I finally relax.

If Bucharest was a battle, then Wembley was a war of attrition. And who better to have alongside you in the trenches than Pat Jennings. I watched the action unfold from the Wembley tunnel alongside my compatriot Alan Green of Radio Five Live, and impartiality went right out the window as we kicked and headed every ball. Pat's goalmouth was frozen in the first half, yet he still managed to tiptoe across to tip away Glenn Hoddle's dipping drive. In the second-half, he miraculously clawed a Kerry Dixon header away from right underneath the crossbar, the moment playing itself out as if in slow motion.

If that wasn't enough, the big man also found the time and presence of mind to influence England's tactics. Dixon was an orthodox type of centre-forward and was getting little change from our defence. As the game reached the final quarter, the Chelsea player landed heavily just outside our 18-yard box. Pat noticed Tony Woodcock warming up on the touch-line and ambled out of his goal, apparently to offer some words of sympathy to the stricken striker. Of course, our Pat was a lot shrewder than that. He knew Woodcock's pace could trouble our tiring rearguard, so he leaned over and whispered to

Dixon that he'd better get up because Woodcock was ready to replace him. Before you could say 'magic sponge', Dixon was back on his feet.

When the final whistle blew with the score at 0–0, Alan and I hugged and jumped up and down like schoolkids after a chocolate overload. I was still a gibbering wreck when it came to conducting the post-match interviews. When I came to edit the material the following day, I cringed at my high-pitched dialogue with Ray Wilkins. I'd met the Manchester United midfielder before; in fact he'd been very hospitable to my son Darren during a visit to Old Trafford. What the poor man must have thought as I fired questions at him like some over-energised novice. But what the hell, we'd done it again. Amazingly, little Northern Ireland was heading to the exotic climes of Mexico.

It was my second World Cup, both as a reporter and as a training-ground replacement for the walking wounded. Although I was 43 by this time, I could still get about the park and even on the odd occasion make an impression. At the end of one session, Nottingham Forest's David Campbell, a supremely fit lad nicknamed 'Road Runner', looked over and said, 'Do you ever give the bloody ball away?' I took that as a real compliment. Now, don't get me wrong, I was no midfield maestro. In fact, more often than not, I got a timely reminder of my limitations. I found Dee McCreery, for example, almost impossible to cope with, his tenacious tackling and incredible work rate simply overpowering.

But if there was a single moment that illustrated the point, it was my one-on-one with Pat. A neat one-two on the edge of the box brought me close enough to see the whites of the big man's eyes. Preparing to pull the trigger, I thought, 'Wait until I tell the boys back home I scored against Pat Jennings.' No sooner had the notion flashed across my mind than my confidence shattered into a thousand pieces. In that millisecond of distraction, the reality of the situation hit home. So, instead of having a go, I side-footed the ball into the path of the on-rushing Billy Hamilton. Yes, I'd bottled it. That was bad enough, but Billy only goes and twists the knife by blasting the ball wide. I could have done that well enough myself. I know it might sound childish, but I still think about that chance. I'm still kicking myself for not shooting.

It was Sammy McIlroy's thoughtfulness that helped me snap out of my surly mood. He'd witnessed my shot-shy antics, and back at the team hotel he announced at the top of his voice, 'They can talk all they want, but for me you were our Man of the Match.' It was a lovely touch. As I revelled in my pre-eminent position, Billy Bingham arrived and asked for a word with Sammy. His mother had just died. I went to see Sammy before he flew home. He was sitting outside his room, still trying to come to terms with the news. I would discover later in life how devastating the loss of your mother can be, but back then I could only imagine his pain. Sammy returned to training in New Mexico after the funeral in Manchester, which was typical of a man who always demonstrated total commitment to the cause. That's one of the reasons I found his experience as Northern Ireland's manager so cruel. Sammy couldn't have bought a goal, let alone a win, during his tenure. If only some members of his Northern Ireland squad had shown half of his devotion, it could have been so different. He deserved better from them.

With my Man-of-the-Match performance under my belt, I was surely in line for that elusive first cap. I mean, Billy didn't have to play me in a World Cup match, but at least the manager could see his way to handing me a start in the friendly he'd arranged with Scotland. It was one of the more bizarre fixtures in the history of either country: an unofficial international between Northern Ireland and Scotland at a university campus in New Mexico. Alex Ferguson was in charge of the Scots, having taken over from Jock Stein, who, tragically, had collapsed and died during the World Cup qualifier with Wales at Ninian Park in Cardiff. Between them, Bingie and Fergie hatched the plan, no doubt realising the relative proximity of their respective training headquarters allowed for the possibility of much-needed competitive action.

Of course, I didn't make the squad, although I'm sure Billy thought long and hard about his decision to leave me out. But if I wasn't going to earn my international spurs against the Scots, I could at least renew my friendship with Graeme Souness. We had got to know each other thanks to promotional work for Ronnie Field, owner of a Saab dealership in Northern Ireland. On one occasion, we teamed up for the Shankill Road Liverpool Supporters Club Player of the Year dinner. Graeme and I shared the top table with the then Lord Mayor of Belfast, Tommy Patton, and his good lady. It was the pocket-sized chairman of the Belfast club who introduced me, with that sharp local intonation. 'You'll all know this man, he's aff the bax,' he announced. Our host went on to inform the rather rowdy gathering that he was ad libbing, adding for those unsure of the terminology, 'That's with no notes nor nathing.' Unfortunately, this Shankill shortstop made the mistake of starting his next sentence with, 'I'm standing here . . .' That was as far as the next sentence progressed before some wag heckled, 'Are ye?' The wee man waited for the laughter to subside, then calmly said, 'I know who said that. I'll deal with you afterwards.' I wouldn't like to have been in that bloke's shoes.

And speaking of footwear, that's exactly what Graeme and I found to talk about as we waited for the speeches to take their course. In fact, you could say we became sole-mates. I complimented the mustachioed midfielder on his stylish patent-leather shoes. No sooner had I mentioned the slip-ons than he slipped one of them off and suggested I try it for size, adding that a Scouse mate of his could get them at a knock-down price. 'I'll get you a pair,' he said. Sure enough, two weeks later a pair of shiny shoes arrived for yours truly. They turned out to be another source of ammunition for my mucker Gerry Kelly, who seemingly never failed to notice that I was wearing the 'Souness shoes', as he called them. Graeme subsequently moved from Anfield to Sampdoria in Italy. Our paths crossed again, and I mentioned that the shoes were still going strong. With what appeared to be genuine regret, Graeme said I should have given him a call. 'The shoes in Italy are great,' he enthused, 'I could have sent you a few pairs.' I've no doubt he would have, too, but can you imagine the call? 'Hello, could I speak to Graeme Souness? How's it going, Graeme? It's Jackie Fullerton. I know we haven't spoken for a while, but any chance of a couple of pairs of Italian loafers?' Nah, I don't think so.

It's funny how things turn out. In the past couple of years, Graeme Souness has gone from being a mate to a major source of inspiration. When I had my heart bypass operation in 2004, it was Graeme's success in overcoming the same procedure in 1992 that lifted the gloom. The fact that he had made a speedy return to the stressful environment of management and was still able to take an active part in training was just what I needed to focus on. Graeme even sent me a thoughtful get-well-soon message.

I suppose his kind gesture shouldn't have surprised me. There's a humanity and magnanimity in him that sit slightly uneasily with the hard-man image. That generosity of spirit manifested itself quite literally at a Liverpool versus Stoke City match I was working on for UTV. I spent the morning on the training ground, moved on to the match and was obviously feeling the pace when I finished my interview with Liverpool's manager. 'Long day?' Graeme enquired, having sensed my batteries were running low. 'I bet you could kill for a vodka and Diet Coke?' He told me to go into the players' lounge and he would join me as soon as he could. I voiced my concern about gaining admission to Anfield's inner sanctum. 'I think you might have a chance,' Graeme joked, 'I'm the manager.' Unfortunately for me, that same manager had imposed some restrictions on the sale of alcohol in the lounge, with beer and wine the only alternative to soft drinks. My vodka would have to wait. I'm not a great fan of wine or beer, so I was sipping rather pathetically on a Diet Coke when a steward called from over my shoulder, 'Are you Mr Fullerton?' He then handed me a large Smirnoff and Diet Coke and a tray of sandwiches. 'I think you'll find something there to your taste, just don't tell anyone, though.' I asked where it had come from and was told from the manager's office. 'Mr Souness wanted to make sure you were all right.'

Scotland won the match against Northern Ireland in New Mexico 5–2, and Terry Smyth won his battle with the IFA for the right to film it. They were anxious to keep it behind closed doors, but Terence was determined that such an unusual home international should make it onto our television screens in some form. Star of the show was undoubtedly Arsenal's Charlie Nicholas. He scored two and was a constant thorn in the side of the Northern Ireland defence with his touch and vision. It's easy to forget just how talented a player he was. With regular substitutions interrupting the flow, no one read too much into that defeat. However, it did provide a measure of insight into the fate that awaited us in Mexico. The nucleus of the '82 squad was still intact, but they were now four years older. In the heat and altitude, it was going to be tough.

There were two birthdays celebrated in the Northern Ireland camp during the 1986 World Cup, one slightly more significant than the other. John Alexander Fullerton, reporter and part-time squad member, turned 43 on 22 May, the occasion marked by another breach of Bingham's rules. This time, there were UTV's charismatic cameraman Albert Kirk, some members of the media and a group of players that included Pat Jennings, Gerry Armstrong, Billy Hamilton and John McClelland. Terry Smyth had learned his lesson in Spain, and stayed behind to provide the get-out-of-jail-free card, if necessary. His thinking was that, if I was caught, he could publicly reprimand me in front of Billy. That might be enough to save us from expulsion. The rest of us slipped into three taxis which we had arranged to have sitting at the back entrance of the hotel, behind the tennis courts. Unfortunately, the one-way system in the sprawling complex meant we had to pass by the front entrance in order to leave. We all crouched down, suppressing the giggles, as the trio of yellow cabs rumbled past. Our destination was a ranch party we had been invited to by some local girls.

It proved to be a bit of an eye-opener for me. I was sitting in a room, minding my own business, when a girl asked would I like a cigarette. Glancing at the packet on the table next to me, I thanked her and declined. 'No! Would you like a *cigarette*,' she repeated. Finally, the penny dropped. It wasn't an invitation to chat over a Marlboro; this young lady was offering to share a Jamaican Woodbine, a joint, a spliff. 'No thanks,' I said. She looked at me as if I was the biggest square in the chess club and left. A few minutes later, as I was talking to Gerry and Pat, she returned, eyes like saucers and clearly on another planet. It was my first real encounter with drug-taking. I'm not taking any high moral ground here, in fact I will admit that apprehension rather than any antipathy made me refuse her offer. As someone who smoked and clearly had an addictive personality, my greatest fear was that I might actually like it.

If my birthday was all about a few relaxing beers and a bite of grub, big Pat's was an infinitely more stimulating affair. For fate conspired to make his final appearance in an international jersey, in any jersey, coincide with his 41st birthday. Of course, what could be more fitting for a genuine great than to mark his farewell with a match against the team synonymous with the 'beautiful game', the mighty Brazil?

Emotions were running high, and even the Brazilian fans seemed to embrace the significance of Pat's send-off. Unlike in Spain in '82, there was no prospect of us progressing; this was all about pride and providing a fitting finale to a fabulous career. From the moment of his international debut, in 1964 against Wales at Swansea City's Vetch Field (George Best also earned his first cap that afternoon), Pat Jennings had been a veritable rock. It hadn't all been plain sailing. How could it have been when he was the last line of defence for a small nation like ours? Perhaps the lowest point came in April 1977, when we lost 5–0 to West Germany and the *Belfast Telegraph* headline read: 'Auf Wiedersen, Pat'. It hurt big Pat, although I think it's fair to say he had the last laugh. Between that story and his retirement, he managed to win two FA Cups and a European Cup-Winners' Cup, play in two World Cups and register a world record for international caps. Now he was facing Zico, Socrates, Junior and co. in a heroic last hurrah.

We lost 3–0 to Brazil. But for Pat, it would have been double that. There was nothing he could do about any of the goals, particularly the vicious, swerving wonder strike by Josimar Pereira. Pat told me he was giving a talk at a school in Tottenham recently. During the question-and-answer session, one of the children asks, 'Mr Jennings, how did you feel in the 1986 World Cup when the Brazilian full-back lobbed you?' Pat said he suppressed the urge to say, 'If that was a lob, son . . .' and just smiled. There was a marvellous ovation as Pat Jennings walked off the pitch in Guadalajara. The big man even managed to wave back a couple of times, a fairly animated display by Pat's standards. When I arrived in the dressing-room, the players were still getting changed, and it was the usual hive of activity until I started my interview. Out of respect for Pat and, I suspect, because they too wanted to know what he had to say, the other players fell almost completely silent. We chatted as we had so many times before, only this time I concluded by saying, 'Pat, on behalf of football fans, Northern Ireland fans in particular, can I say, for 22 years of top-class service, thank you and well done.' As each word rolled off my tongue, the lump in my throat grew bigger. It was a moment I'll never forget. For so long, Pat Jennings had been there to save the day, a colossus who could send a pulse of confidence through his team with one of his trademark one-handed takes. It felt like he would go on for ever. None of us wanted to accept that he couldn't.

Pat's retirement brought the curtain down on an incredible decade for Northern Ireland international football. Billy Bingham had many advantages over his modern counterparts, not least the fact that many of his squad plied their trade in the English league's top flight. But that should not be allowed to detract from the extraordinary way he made them gel as a group. His teams were set up in a way that made them difficult to break down; he asked players to recreate the roles they performed at club level; and he instilled a positive mental state in which anything seemed possible. That approach secured two British Home Championships, stunning home and away victories over West Germany and appearances at two successive World Cup finals. During a troubled time in this country's history, his teams gave us something to cheer. Peter Doherty would have been proud. There's a wall outside Windsor Park daubed with what can only be described as a supporters' Hall of Fame. Amongst the painted faces that peer down at fans as they make their way into the old stadium are Best, Blanchflower and Bingham. If I had a pound for every time someone has said the Bingham image looks like me!

Northern Ireland's first training camp in the furnace-like heat of Guadalajara proved to be quite an attraction. It was the combination of sharing a group with Brazil and the appearance of Norman Whiteside, the man who four years earlier had broken Pelé's record. I was wearing a tracksuit top and shorts, ready, as always, in case Billy required my services. Some of the players were limbering up and I was nattering to Malcolm Brodie when all hell broke loose. Suddenly, I was surrounded, the stampeding journalists screaming 'Bingham! Bingham!' I felt like Custer at Little Big Horn as I tried to explain that it was a case of mistaken identity. Somehow, though, my meaning was getting lost in translation. Finally, I turned to Malcolm for help. I looked at him, he looked at me, but it was a little Mexican reporter who spoke first. He stared forlornly at Malky, then pleaded, 'He Meestar *Bing*ham?' placing the emphasis on the 'Bing' in the way Manuel from *Fawlty Towers* might. 'No!' Malcolm fired back with no little force. But the wee man was having none of it: '*Si, señor!*' At this stage, Malcolm is determined to make himself understood, so, in that wonderfully gruff Glaswegian burr, he barks, 'That's not Bingham. He's not a coach, he's a singer!' Lord knows over the years I've often wished *that* were true.

Chapter Seven

A SONG IN MY HEART

My uncle, Willie Kernohan, was centre stage as always. Larger than life, 'Lar', as everyone in Harryville affectionately knew him, could best be described as a one-man amusement arcade. Compère, comedian and singer-in-chief, big Lar treated the Raglan Bar's microphone like his own private property. To be honest, he didn't really need any electronic enhancement to be heard. Uncle Willie's thunderous voice matched his extrovert personality, decibel-counter needles dancing in and out of the red when he spoke or warbled. 'Seen and not heard' was a maxim he set little store by. You couldn't help but like Lar; in fact, he was one of the reasons I was so looking forward to post-match drinks at the Raglan. I'd arranged to meet up with my dad after playing for Ballymena United in the afternoon. Of course, he and a few other family members were feeling no pain by the time I arrived, having spent the match day flitting between bar and bookie's shop. It had all the ingredients for an entertaining evening. What I didn't realise was that my uncle had decided I was also going to be part of the entertainment.

Lar was about five songs into his latest set when the heckling really took hold – good-natured stuff, mind, because you didn't mess with my Uncle Willie. We jokingly called him John Wayne, for it seemed this tough former Desert Rat had single-handedly won the war. Lar had a lengthy catalogue of wartime yarns and he loved nothing better than to poke fun at those of us who likened him to 'the Duke'. 'Son,' he would say, with a glint in his eye, 'Hitler was out one night, Rommel by his side, looking up at the sky. Rommel said, "Mein Führer, there's a shooting star!" Hitler thumped him on the arm and said, "Never mind the shooting star, just capture big Lar!"'

Fortunately for this late-afternoon audience, the Nazis' greatest nemesis was in amenable mood. Clearly deciding there was no point fighting the inevitable, Lar relinquished the spotlight. He'd soon manoeuvre his way back to the mike, but for now it was time to find a suitable support act. 'Let's hear a song from Jack,' came the shout, for my father, too, was no stranger to this singing lark. But Lar had other ideas. 'No,' he said. 'Rather than Jack Senior, let's hear from Jack Junior.' Sure, I liked to sing, but not in a packed bar with only the local barber (Willie's brother George) on accordion as accompaniment. As I made my way between the tables, trying to remember the words to 'Green Green Grass of Home', another Raglan regular voiced his concern. 'Can young Jackie sing?' he enquired. Lar's answer came with a hefty dollop of disdain: 'What do you mean, can Jackie sing? Isn't he a Fullerton? All the bloody Fullertons can sing.' He was right, all the Fullertons could.

Dad loved to sing, the local golf club's 19th hole his favourite location for an impromptu performance. He wasn't the only family member who liked to exercise the larynx. Aunt Bella could bring a tear to a navvy's eye with her rendition of 'Bonnie

Kellswater', Uncle Tom was a mainstay of the choir in Connor, Uncle Alex sang in a male-voice chorus and, of course, there was Uncle Willie. My sister, Mareen, and brother, Jimmy, both played professionally in bands. Best of the lot, though, was my mum. Martha Fullerton was a beautiful singer, yet she shunned almost every invitation to display those dulcet tones. It used to drive my father to distraction. Mum didn't have the same desire to perform that coursed through our veins; she was happiest at home just singing along to 'No Other Love' by Yorkshire's romantic balladeer Ronnie Hilton, Frankie Vaughan's 'Give Me the Moonlight, Give Me the Girl' or tunes from *The Great Caruso* by tenor turned Hollywood movie star Mario Lanza. Not surprisingly, I was influenced by the sounds around me. Even today, if there's a rerun of *The Student Prince*, an MGM movie with actor Edmund Purdom miming to Lanza's magnificent vocals, you couldn't prise me from the armchair with a crowbar. Music was part of life in the Fullerton family; it's become part of who I am.

If it hadn't been for football, I might well have followed my brother and sister in making music more than just a hobby. I did combine the two for a while in my late teens, although it did little for my street cred. It was Jimmy who persuaded me to join the ranks of the Harold Alexander Male Voice Chorus. I was soon a willing convert. Before long, I was happily donning the warpaint for the black and white minstrel shows we did in conjunction with the local ladies' chorus, led by soloist Lorna Hughes. These collaborations – the Harold Alexander Concerts – played to packed houses up and down the country, the girls helping to guide us through the choreographed dance routines. I was no Fred Astaire, but I managed to hold my own. As it turned out, it wasn't a quickstep that caught me out, it was just one step too far on the grand elevated stage in Ballymena's Town Hall. To make matters worse, my mates were sitting smugly in the audience. They already regarded my participation in the show as a bit 'girlie' and I suppose they did have a point. For, if you were creating a look to impress a teenager in the '50s, it was unlikely to include make-up, white trousers, shoes and gloves, and a candy-striped blazer, topped off with a straw boater.

And if that wasn't ammunition enough for some serious urine extraction, I decided to put my foot in it at the most inopportune moment. Well, not so much my foot as my left leg. It was right in the middle of my mimed Al Jolson solo, just as I was telling the good folks of Ballymena how much I loved 'My Mammy'. Arms spread apart, I went down on bended knee to plead to the dear old bird. Unfortunately, as I attempted to get up, my knee locked. I tried again – no joy. Still goldfishing to Jolson, my panic growing by the second, I gave it another shot. Miraculously, my knee freed itself and I carried on with the concert, the audience seemingly oblivious to my dilemma. It was only after the show that I realised my faux pas hadn't gone completely unnoticed. As my mates gathered round backstage, one of them casually asked, 'By the way, who was that old man doing the miming who couldn't get up?'

I could have folded under peer pressure, but the truth was that I enjoyed everything about the Harold Alexander experience, not least the camaraderie. We went on tour to the south of Scotland, playing three dates in Castle Douglas, arranged through my Uncle Robert (Hamill), a church minister. And I'll never forget the winter night in 1963 at Lurgan Town Hall. A few of us blokes had nipped into the lounge bar during the interval for a shandy. As we wet our whistles, a newsflash announced that President Kennedy had been assassinated. By the time we returned to the main auditorium, reports of JFK's murder had spread like wildfire.

Singing pandered to the performer in me, or maybe it would be more accurate to say the show-off in me. But then, so too did flying along the left wing with the ball at my feet and a full-back breathing down my neck. As my Irish League career developed, it became clear that time, or rather the lack of it, would prevent me from having the best of both worlds. However, it didn't rule out the occasional guest appearance. If I felt the need to indulge the singer in me, I only had to turn up at one of Jimmy's gigs. My sibling invariably invited his little bro to join him for a few Everly Brothers harmonies, a dalliance with the business that only reinforced my rose-tinted vision. I envied Jimmy when he took to the stage with Pendil or The Red Admirals. 'You're lucky doing this,' I once told my brother after we'd performed a couple of numbers. He didn't quite see it that way. Jimmy pointed out the difference between the reality and my romantic perception of a musician's life – all adrenalin rush and adulation. He explained that when you're lugging gear into a van in the early hours of the morning three nights a week in all weathers, it's a bit of a passion-killer. Of course, I could pick and choose when I wanted to perform. For Jimmy – and Mareen, who sang for many years with Cuddles, one of the Causeway Coast's most popular and hard-working groups – there was no such luxury.

Between the '50s and the '70s, some 500 bands, playing music reflecting the popular songs of the day and often including a number of covers in their sets, were showcased on the vibrant showband scene in Ireland. Five nights a week, these musical missionaries travelled the length and breadth of the Emerald Isle, preaching to the converted in packed ballrooms and dance-halls. One of the best local exponents of the showband craft was The Freshmen. Fronted by Billy Brown and Derek Dean, who co-wrote the Ballymena band's new material, they were renowned for their fantastic harmonies. Not so long ago, I bumped into another member of the band in the supermarket. Torry McGahey was a bloke I always admired. Having left the music scene he went back to school, completing his O and A Levels as a mature student. Recently retired from teaching, Torry's now back on the road again with an Eagles tribute band, The Illeagles. Years of listening to other people's attempts at making music had made him realise his own talent. Having been bitten by the musical bug as a teenager, it was almost inevitable he would return to the scene.

We long for our lost youth just a little, whether it's the disco-dancing, flare-wearing '70s or the electro-pop and eyeliner of the '80s. For me, it was the showband era and nights out at The Flamingo. My local haunt was just one of many on the circuit. On any given evening north of the border you could stomp at The Savoy in Portadown or party in Portaferry's Locarno. Then there was The Star in Omagh, Caproni's in Bangor, The Embassy in Derry, The Strand in Portstewart and Portrush's Arcadia Ballroom, opened in 1953 with a set by Dave Glover and his band, who became residents there. Belfast boasted The Boom Boom Rooms on Arthur Street, as well as The Orpheus, The Gala, The Orchid and Maxim's to name but a few. The punters had one thing in common: they all worshipped at the showband altar. I spent more time staring at the star names, like Dickie Rock, Brendan Bowyer, Joe Dolan and Butch Moore, than I did dancing to their music. These guys knew how to work a room, how to wow a crowd, and I couldn't help hankering after some of that hero-worship for myself.

I'm a guy who loves to sing. I'm not a great singer, but I can carry a tune. Basically, I'm a crooner. My brother Jimmy and I have similar singing styles and, for that matter, musical taste. Over the years, I've liked an eclectic enough mix of music, everything from The Beatles to Billy Fury, The Rolling Stones to Oasis. But for Jimmy and me, there's really only one thing that truly floats our boat. Pennsylvanian Perry Como, former prizefighter Dean Martin and the silky-smooth Nat 'King' Cole are the sort of singers that move us. They may seem middle of the road compared to today's gangsta rappers, but they were actually anything but. When it comes to hell-raising and courting controversy, look no further than 'Ol' Blue Eyes' himself, Francis Albert Sinatra. 'The Chairman of the Board' certainly did things his way. He drank, womanised, socialised with mafia mobsters, and still had the ability to turn it on when the spotlight shone. It was a teammate at Ballymena Cricket Club who turned me on to Sinatra's laid-back style. I was just 16 when John Shields asked, 'Do you like Sinatra?'

'Nah,' I told him.

'You will.'

John sowed the seed, and by the time my teens turned to twenties, I too was hooked on the man from Hoboken. In 2006, I had the opportunity to visit the house on Monroe Street in Hoboken, New Jersey, where Sinatra was born. It was during Northern Ireland's American tour, and I found the experience a genuine thrill. Jimmy and I both regret that we never had the chance to see the leader of the Rat Pack perform live in concert. We did, however, have front-row seats for another of our musical idols.

It was the summer of 1977 and the brothers Fullerton were having it large on holiday in Las Vegas. We were surprised, and delighted, to find seats available for Andy Williams' concert at that entertainment Mecca, Caesars Palace. Slipping a $10 bill into the appropriate palm moved us closer to the stage, and we slipped into our seats near the front. Trying not to look like two green-as-the-grass country boys, Jimmy and I sat transfixed, eyes firmly on the stage in front of us. Suddenly, there was a flash of light. Then, about ten yards to our left, Andy Williams appeared from the floor, perched on a moving plinth and wearing a pearly-white suit. For the next two hours, he went through his full repertoire with flawless ease, the hairs on my neck standing to attention. 'Moon River' was majestic, 'Can't Get Used to Losing You' nothing short of superb, 'Where Do I Begin' quite brilliant. When we returned to the bright lights of the Strip, Jimmy and I reflected on what we'd witnessed. For both of us, it was something of a reality check. For a member of a band, like Jimmy, and for me, a wannabe singer, there was the realisation of a yawning gap between what we did and what Williams could do. We vowed to return to Las Vegas. Maybe next time we would really hit the jackpot and Sinatra or Presley would be the main act in town. At least half of that dream was shattered within a matter of weeks. Elvis was dead.

I've been fortunate enough to see Andy Williams sing live on two other occasions. Linda and I caught his act in Manchester in '79 and again more recently at the Waterfront Hall in Belfast. Williams, by that time a man of 70, was still sublime. He may have taken one or two notes down an octave or two, but his voice was crystal clear. As we made our way back to the car, still in awe of the man's timeless talent, I said to Linda, 'You know the way I fancy myself as a bit of a singer? Well, I think it's time to hang up the mike.' We do have something in common, Andy and I. For Mr 'Moon River' isn't the only old hand to have warbled at the Waterfront. Thanks to musician and broadcaster George Jones, I was able to experience the thrill of playing to an audience in that awesome auditorium. George – a fine entertainer, first with his group Clubsound, then as a solo performer – had recruited my services on a number of occasions for charity golf events. I played in the Johnny Mathis Classic and in a Norman Wisdom event at Royal Portrush. Needless to say, I was thinking swinging rather than singing when he said to me one afternoon in 2002, 'I've got a gig for you, I know you'll enjoy it.' The first inkling I had that this did not involve a driver and a set of irons was when he added, 'I know you can do it.' George explained that he was putting on a '50s songbook show, the slight drawback (for me, anyway) being that it was live at the Waterfront.

I was standing in the wings, a chain-smoking wreck. This wasn't the golf club or the local bar, where Dutch courage could be used to moisten the lips and oil the tonsils. This was the most sobering experience of my life. George gave a potted history of the artist, then announced to the audience: 'Singing the songs of Dean Martin, please welcome, from BBC Sport, Jackie Fullerton!' One deep breath and out I went. As the applause rang out, my mind went totally blank. I couldn't remember the song, I couldn't remember the key, and I sure as hell couldn't remember the words. Then the orchestra struck its first note. In that instant, everything fell into place. Suddenly, I could hear the music, find the key and recall every word. My first song was a bit breathless, but the warmth of the applause gave me the impetus to go on. My psychological crutch had been that the crowd would cut me some slack because they knew I was Jackie off the telly, not a professional singer. They were proving me right. I completed three Deano numbers, then three by Perry Como in the second half of the show. The experience was all that I had ever dreamed of, and more. The orchestra, under the guidance of the show's musical director Crawford Bell, was inspiring, the backing singers uplifting, the acoustics stunning. It was one of the most exhilarating episodes of my life.

If that night at the Waterfront remains the pinnacle, coming a close second and third would be singing for country superstar Charley Pride and an operatic opus of epic proportions for *Children in Need*. It was a home-grown country boy, Hugo Duncan, who invited me to sing on his television series *Hugo and Friends*, to be recorded in BBC Northern Ireland's Blackstaff Studios. As if the pressure of the cameras wasn't enough, the audience included Foster & Allen, Dennis Locorriere, the former lead singer with Dr Hook, and the star of the show, Charley Pride, who was sitting at a table directly in front of the stage. I was pleased with my performance that night, but ecstatic when I learned it had also met with the approval of the man who had ascended from a Mississippi cotton farm to the Country Music Hall of Fame. I bumped into the legendary Mr Pride just after finishing a short interview with Hugo. I was initially impressed that he remembered my name. 'Jackie,' he said in that warm southern drawl, 'you're a fine singer with a sweet voice.' Now that's what I call a compliment. He might not have realised it, but Charley Pride had just made me the proudest man on the planet.

My association with *Children in Need* night began only a few months after I joined the BBC. (I had Jim Neilly to thank for taking my career in a new direction. Jim, then Head of Sport at BBC NI, lured me to Broadcasting House with a financial offer no self-respecting Ballymena man could refuse.) It was late February 1992 when Fidelma Harkin, a youth-programme producer, first approached me. Expecting a sporting request, perhaps for a contact number for some youth football team, I was taken aback when she asked me to co-host the *Children in Need* programme with Eurovision Song Contest winner Linda Martin. My first thought was of the toes I might be treading on if I accepted this offer so soon after my switch from UTV. I was assured that the usual presenters, Wendy Austin and Sean Rafferty, had no problems stepping aside. Both were extremely magnanimous. Sean, in particular, proved to me that he was not only a fine broadcaster but also a fine man. If his nose was put out of joint in any way, he certainly didn't show it. In fact, he was gracious enough to wish me good luck just before we went on air.

As it turned out, I needed it. The difficulty with this particular show is its unpredictability. Dovetailing with the network output fronted by the mercurial Mr Wogan was not always easy. It was a case of hitting junctions, although it didn't always go according to plan. At one point, I linked across to London only to be told in my earpiece that they weren't ready. There was nothing else for it, so I decided to sing. I was nearing the end of that old favourite of mine, 'Green Green Grass of Home', when my producer gave me the green light to link once more to Terry Wogan. When the dust had settled, Gerry Anderson, award-winning broadcaster and razor-sharp raconteur, ambled up to my side. 'Well done,' he said, 'that wasn't easy.' Presenting *Children in Need* can be incredibly challenging, especially if the evening's producer happens to be Alex Johnston. There are no safe options taken when he's around, an approach that can often bring out the best in you. It wasn't enough for Alex that my BBC colleague and friend Lata Sharma and I were to perform a Rod Stewart and Tina Turner-style duet, it had to be live. Lata and I were still learning the words of that classic Marvin Gaye/Kim Weston number 'It Takes Two' as George Jones introduced us. Trying to remember the words would become a recurring theme for me on *Children in Need* night, never more so than on the evening I was the warm-up act for Westlife.

So you're planning the show's line-up. Who do you get to go on before the biggest boy band in music, a handsome quintet with a hatful of number one records? Answer: a trio of ageing broadcasters dressed up to look like The Three Tenors. My old mate from UTV Gerry Kelly was our Pavarotti (he'll love me for saying that), with Gerry Anderson and myself completing this classical collaboration to die for. Being consummate professionals, we decided to pore over the lyrics as they poured us a few drinks. There was plenty of laughter and reminiscing, but little learning. In fact, it was very relaxed until we glanced at the clock. Stepping out to sing, I had the words shoved into my pocket and Gerry A. was still holding them in his hand. It was a far from flawless rendition of Gershwin's 'Stand Up and Fight', but it went down a storm.

Backstage, we were on cloud nine. Gerry Kelly was so taken by the whole thing, he wanted to sing it again.

It was pure adrenalin, something my wife has often struggled to understand. She appreciates most facets of the business, and no one could be more supportive, especially in the face of any criticism. Yet when it comes to that natural rush, and in particular its lingering effects, she has never quite got her head around it. Often, after live television, I feel sharp as a tack even on the drive home, replaying in my mind every incident, every line of commentary. A large vodka and Diet Coke may not seem the ideal nightcap – it never has to Linda – but it is my way of taking the edge off that buzz. Am I confessing to being some sort of adrenalin junkie? Well, maybe I wouldn't go quite that far, but there is a craving at work there. People who like to perform invariably find a way of doing just that. Even on holiday, a fix is never too far away.

Majorca and music go hand in hand, at least for me they do. For many years, Linda and I have sat in The Stadium, a piano bar in Palma Nova, relaxing to the sweet soul sounds of The Platters and The Drifters. I'm not always quite so passive. Just as I did all those years ago with Jimmy, I started to make occasional guest appearances with one of the island's cabaret entertainers, a Liverpudlian called Lee J. Allen. A fine keyboard player, Lee was the resident act at The Rover's Return in Santa Ponsa. The Rover's proved popular with Scottish and Ulster folk, and it didn't escape Lee's attention that I was being asked to sign autographs and pose for pics. Before I knew it, he had persuaded me to perform a full show. Posters appeared advertising the night, the sight of them sending me into a cold sweat. You see, it had dawned on me that I only actually knew about five songs. I could sing the verse and perhaps a chorus of many more, but that wasn't going to cut it in front of an expectant holiday crowd. Fortunately no one seemed to notice my inadequacies and

I decided to quit whilst I was ahead. I never did repeat my one-man show.

However, I did continue to take up Lee's invitation to join him on stage for two or three numbers. It was towards the end of my mini-set one night that I spotted two familiar faces. I remembered Margo Burns from her showband days with Margo and the Marvettes, and I went over for a chat with her and husband Trevor. As it happened, Lee and many of Majorca's other musicians were meeting later in Magaluf for a benefit gig. One of their mates, a Scottish performer called Joss Munro, had fallen from a ladder and broken his ankle. They were hoping to raise a few quid to compensate for his loss of earnings. I invited Margo and Trevor along. In the club, I filled Lee in on Margo's musical background, having already checked with her that she didn't mind being asked to sing. One number was all it took to tear the roof off the place. Margo's magnificent rendition of 'Danny Boy' blew the local musos away, and I sauntered over to Lee feeling rather pleased with myself. 'What about that?' I enquired. Lee paused, then called me a berk.

'What's wrong?' I continued. 'She was brilliant.'

'I know,' he said, 'but who the hell is going to follow that?'

News of Margo's performance spread, and her one-night stand became six nights a week for an entire season. Some 16 years on, and she is still going strong. Margo and Trevor spend May until October in Santa Ponsa, the rest of the time they live in Donaghadee. A few years back, they appeared on Gerry Kelly's chat show. He asked how the Majorca connection had come about, and Margo recounted the story, thanking me on air for the introduction. Being a good Ballymena man, I've often thanked them for thanking me, whilst at the same time enquiring about my percentage.

Majorca or Mexico, I'll sing before the proverbial hat has hit the floor. During the '86 World Cup in South America, I even managed to become the wedding singer at a posh local soirée. Elton Welsby and I had been peeking at a traditional Mexican wedding taking place in our hotel. The bride's family brought us in and gave us seats on the periphery of proceedings. Unbeknown to me, Elton informed the parents that Jackie was a good singer. I ended up performing 'My Way' to general acclaim. We retold the events of the day later on to Ron Atkinson. 'Big Ron' fancies himself as the fifth member of the Rat Pack (he's even recorded a CD) and he was green with envy by the time we'd embellished the story to include a couple of standing ovations.

It didn't take much to instigate a sing-song on trips with Northern Ireland. One of the most memorable was after beating West Germany in November 1983. Back at Hamburg's Atlantic Hotel the band played 'Danny Boy' as a tribute. Then Pat Jennings (whose wife, Eleanor, was a showband singer) and Gerry Armstrong led the singing into the wee small hours.

At Irish League games and internationals the fans often chant, 'Jackie, Jackie, give us a song!' And do you know what? I love it. Not everyone, however, is so keen to hear me sing. I met a bloke a few years back at a function. He approached, thrust out a piece of paper and asked me to sign it for his better half.

'It's for the wife,' he grunted. 'She loves you and loves your singing.'

'What's her name?' I asked my less-than-fawning fan.

He told me, and a bit more besides, finishing with: 'Yes, the wife loves you, but personally I can't stand you.'

I'm sure he's not alone. My singing may not be everyone's cup of tea, but I make no apologies for holding a mike. It feels good to sing; like big Lar said, it's what we Fullertons do. Even the grandkids are getting in on the act. I was chuffed to bits last year when my son Darren's twins Erin and Jack (then seven years old) won a school cup for their piano duet. Erin in particular has inherited the singing bug. Crank up the karaoke machine and she'll belt out a Bassey, or copy Celine. She even sings 'My Way'. I wouldn't mind so much, but she does it better than me.

Chapter Eight

TOUCHED BY GENIUS

George took possession of the ball close to the halfway line. With nothing more than a superficial shrug of those slight shoulders, he ghosted past three Turkish players. Just as he swept forward, the ball suddenly seemed to take a hop, and in the blink of an eye Bestie let fly. The crowd inside the ground gave a collective gasp as the shot cannoned off the crossbar, leaving it reverberating like a tuning fork. It all happened with such incredible speed and fantastic fury that I was forced to seek confirmation that it had happened at all. I glanced at my brother Jimmy in the South Stand seat beside me. He gazed back. Neither of us spoke. It was a 'Finney moment'. Five years earlier, on the same Windsor Park sward, I watched Tom Finney play for Lisburn Distillery against the mighty Benfica in the 1963–64 European Cup. The match ended 3–3 and 'The Preston Plumber', then 41 years old and all but retired, was breathtaking. Germano, a Portuguese international centre-half, was close to tears as Tom tormented him with his close control, feints and flicks. It was a genius at work. Now, on 23 October 1968, watching Best in an international against Turkey, I was experiencing that same feeling of awe. I had asked what all the fuss was about, wondered why they called him 'The Wonder Boy'. Now I knew: George Best was touched by genius too.

Every brush with brilliance brings with it a brief moment of clarity. It's that split-second stop-you-in-your-tracks insight into a world where only the privileged few reside. There's seldom any warning, and it can happen in the most unlikely of places; but once you've seen the light, it's as if everything else falls into place. Jurby Airfield, a disused former military facility on the Isle of Man, was the setting for just such an epiphany. It was here that I glimpsed, and finally understood, the true majesty of the man they called 'the King of the Roads'.

Joey Dunlop had asked me along to this impromptu test session because the rest of his team were delayed. We enjoyed a few cigarettes and a chat during the van ride, but the relaxed mood dissipated when he asked for help to unload his bike. Shoving a plank out of the back door, Joey began lowering the gleaming 750cc Honda on which his (and most of the Japanese manufacturer's) hopes for the forthcoming TT races were pinned. My already nervous disposition wasn't helped when Joey cautioned in his Ballymoney brogue: 'Dinnae be droppin' her, or we're sunk.' I was sweating like the proverbial pink farmyard animal as we gradually guided the bike to terra firma, the entire manoeuvre carried out with the sort of tender loving care normally reserved for a carrycot. Of course, no sooner had we finished than the cavalry appeared on the horizon, in the form of Joey's charismatic manager Davy Wood. With the bike fuelled and ready to go, William Joseph Dunlop squeezed into his leathers. He gave a quick blip of the throttle, climbed on, crouched over the tank and scorched up the runway like a jet fighter. Whooosh! It took my breath away. In that instant, as I watched him disappear in a perfunctory puff of exhaust fumes, man and machine were as one.

I've been fortunate enough to meet many of my heroes, but none impressed me more, or tugged harder at my heartstrings, than George and Joey. To catch a glimpse of a genius is one thing, but to be invited inside his private world is something else entirely. George Best and Joey Dunlop afforded me that luxury. In doing so, they gave me the chance to see them with their guard down, to discover that they shared many of the traits that made them great, that the country boy from Armoy and the lad from Belfast's Cregagh estate were not so different after all. I became friends with George and Joey, but it took time. In fact, I was fortunate that first impressions don't in fact count for everything. Technology, or rather my lack of command of it, was to blame for my initial embarrassment in Bestie's case; with Joey, it was a smash-and-grab raid with a microphone.

Joey was just another up-and-coming rider when I first met him in 1975. He was two years away from the first of his record 26 Isle of Man TT wins; I was the same length of time into my television career. Still coming to terms with interviewing and studio presentation, I was a little out of my depth as compère of the prestigious Enkalon Motorcyclist of the Year Awards. I looked the part, although in hindsight turning up wearing a sharp mohair suit probably did little to dispel preconceived notions that I was just some flash git off the television. Linda was always telling me I should take an interest in bikes. Her father David was a fan and had taken her to the North West 200 and the Ulster Grand Prix since childhood. Unfortunately, race meetings clashed with match days, and only when I entered television did I begin to investigate a sport I would eventually grow to love. In '75, though, my knowledge was decidedly sketchy, not the ideal preparation for a room packed with road-racing fanatics.

It was during the question-and-answer session preceding the awards that things began to go pear-shaped. Kick-starting the problems was a punter on the floor who, ignoring the other guests at the top table (motorcycle journalist and broadcaster Harold Crooks, Joey Dunlop, and his brother-in-law and fellow rider Mervyn Robinson), instead directed his question my way. 'Why is there not more motorcycle racing on the television, instead of football and horse racing?' he asked. Cheers, mate, I thought, just the sort of poser you need when your knowledge of sports contracts rivals your knowledge of advanced mathematics. I staggered through some half-cocked notion about people betting on football and horse racing, adding that I felt coverage of motorcycle racing had improved. To tell you the truth, I had no idea whether it had or not. I was just going into public-relations overdrive, assuring him it would continue to improve, when Joey slammed on the brakes.

Leaning across, he grabbed the solitary microphone from my grasp, almost taking my right arm along with it. With his elbow on the table, and fuelled by a wee drink or two, the normally reticent member of the fabled 'Armoy Armada' group of riders announced, 'I would just lik' tae tell Mr Fullerton that I'm no' here tae tawk about football, I'm here tae tawk about bikes.' Pandemonium ensued, and the uproar was just dying down when I reclaimed the mike and said, 'Well, I'd just like to tell Mr Dunlop that I'm here to talk about bikes, too. I was merely trying to answer a question about football and horse racing.' The air crackled. Joseph and I had definitely got off on the wrong foot. We didn't meet again until after the Isle of Man TT of 1977, when Joey took the chequered flag in the Jubilee Classic race, on John Rea's Yamaha. Rea, a local transport manager and road-race sponsor, had bought Joey his first racing bike, a 350 Yamaha, back in 1974.

That summer of '77 I also met George Best for the first time, and in the glamorous setting of Los Angeles to boot. It

HAIR APPARENT
Even at nine months old, that trademark
barnet is beginning to take shape.

SLEMISH SMILES
The Fullerton family outside our prefab
house in Slemish Drive, 1948. That's
dad Jack, mum Martha and my older
brother James. I'm the one with legs like
a sparrow.

TEENAGE KICKS
Joining me (front row, second from left) in the Ballymena Intermediate School XI is
Tommy Aiken (front row, third from right), who went on to play for
Ballymena United and Doncaster Rovers.

THAT TRUSTY LEFT FOOT
Further proof that my right foot was just for standing on. Hugging the left touchline for Glenavon in an Irish League match during the late '60s. (© Eric Cousins)

CRUES CONTROL
The Crusaders team that won the Irish League title in 1972–73. You'll find me in the back row, third from left, and on the extreme left of the front row is my mate, and now Irish League manager, Liam Beckett. (© Chas H. Halliday & Co. Ltd)

TEAM WORK
The sports team at Ulster Television. Standing, from left: Adrian Logan (now Head of Sport at UTV), the legendary Leslie Dawes, some bloke called Fullerton. Seated is my boss, producer, friend and confidant, Terry Smyth.

SHOOTING STAR
Of course, one of the perks of transferring from playing sport to presenting it was having the opportunity to interview football legends like Bobby Charlton.

RIGHT ON CUE
Sporting my entry for the world's largest dickie bow competition during one of the exhibition nights on which I was MC for two-time world snooker champion Alex 'Hurricane' Higgins.

DOUBLE ACT
Do we really look alike? Pictured with the man I used to get mistaken for in foreign climes, former Northern Ireland manager Billy Bingham.

THUMBS UP
Shaking hands with SV Hamburg's Kevin Keegan at the Professional Footballers' Association dinner in London, 1978, the same year he won the first of his two consecutive European Footballer of the Year accolades.
(© *Daily Express*)

THE KING AND I
There was nothing quite like a post-Isle of Man TT homecoming at Joey's Bar in Ballymoney. Here I am pictured with the three Dunlop brothers, Jim (far right), Robert (second right) and Joey (second left). With his arm around the King of the Roads is his 125cc racing sponsor, the late Andy McMenemy. I miss them both. (© John Smith)

A BIRTHDAY HAT-TRICK

Three men, same birthday. Pictured in Los Angeles, 1977. From left: George Best, a 'friend' of Bestie, yours truly and Bobby McAlinden. Remarkably, George, Bobby and I were all born on 22 May.

BEST NIGHT OUT

Linda and I join George and his first wife, Angie, at the Belfast Awards in 1979. Bestie was playing for Hibernian at the time. (© Studio Seven)

AN UNHOLY TRINITY
Best, Law and, er, Fullerton. A proud moment for George and me in 1993: I was privileged to host the occasion of Bestie being given the Freedom of the City by Castlereagh Borough Council. It's all smiles for George, his old mucker Denis Law and me.

DOING IT MY WAY
Everyone knows I'll croon a tune at the drop of a hat.

ROCKIN'
He must be missing his rocking chair, because Val's put his arm around me for support. Pictured with singer Val Doonican and the Flamingo Ballroom promoter Sammy Barr in November 1979.

ON SONG FOR
CHILDREN IN NEED
My *Children In Need* debut in 1992 involved hosting the BBC Northern Ireland programme with Eurovision Song Contest winner Linda Martin.

DRIVING TEST

Ballymena Golf Club captain, Sammy Small, welcomes Ian St John and I to the Raceview course on that bizarre day Bestie went walkabout and a guy appeared through a hole in the hedge.

IN SAFE HANDS

Two of my favourite folk: legendary Northern Ireland goalkeeper Pat Jennings and my producer, mentor and friend, the late Derek Murray. Also pictured is Pat's charming wife Eleanor.

TWO JACKS AND A GOAL-SCORING ACE

Big Jack had clearly forgotten about our row in Orlando. Pictured at a Milk Cup dinner with the England World Cup-winner turned Republic of Ireland World Cup manager, and Northern Ireland goal-scoring legend, now assistant manager, Gerry Armstrong. (© Harrison Photography)

A REAL GENTLE-MANN

One of the most charming men I've ever met, former German international striker, now international manager, Jurgen Klinsmann. I've had the pleasure of interviewing Herr Klinsmann on a number of occasions, including a chat on the boardwalk outside his American home.

A KNIGHT TO REMEMBER
Sir Alex Ferguson and me at a Milk Cup dinner. I'm privileged to be the only person from the BBC Sir Alex will give an interview to.

MAN AND BHOY
Martin O'Neill has proved himself to be a great man, on and off the football field.

CHILD'S PLAY
My grandchildren, twins Jack (left) and Erin, on whom I dote.

was a working holiday of sorts. The plan was for my brother Jimmy and I to spend three weeks seeing the sights stateside and, during the trip, contrive a meeting with the player we'd watched together from the terraces of Windsor. UTV had no radio outlet, so I approached BBC producer Brian Dempster with the idea of me interviewing George, who was then playing for the Los Angeles Aztecs in a vibrant North American Soccer League. Commission secured, I borrowed a tape recorder and blagged Bestie's LA phone number from his dad Dickie, whom I'd met on a few occasions. A couple of days after we arrived on the West Coast, I gave George a call. Bestie explained he would be out of town for the next three days (they had a match in New York) but that we could hook up when he returned.

On a picture postcard Californian morning, we made our way to the Aztecs training ground, two boys from Ballymena barely able to contain their excitement at meeting a sporting legend. Gradually, though, our enthusiasm waned. Ten minutes passed, then twenty, then half an hour; still no sign of Bestie. At three-quarters of an hour, Jimmy and I are at each other's throats. He's threatening to leave, and I'm telling him to relax, we're on holiday. Then I see this guy in the distance coming towards us. I said to Jimmy excitedly, 'There he is, there's George now.' It was the long hair that fooled me. It wasn't George at all, but his best mate Bobby McAlinden. He and George had first met when they were young wingers at Manchester City and Manchester United respectively. Kindred spirits, I suppose you'd call them. They even shared the same birthday. 'Are you Jackie?' Bobby enquired. 'George didn't train today, but he's at Bestie's. Come with me.' Window down, music playing, Bobby drives us in his Pontiac Trans Am to Bestie's bar and restaurant in Hermosa Beach.

It was a surreal experience in many ways, that first sighting of George Best in the flesh. Sure, I'd seen pictures of him,

I knew he was a fashion icon and ladies' man, but was he really that good looking? The answer was yes, and then some. George greeted us wearing frayed cut-off denim shorts and a pair of trainers. He was bronzed, in fantastic physical shape, his raven hair was shining, and, when he smiled, those baby-blue eyes seemed to slice right through to your very soul. In short, he was devastatingly handsome. Little wonder, I thought to myself, that women were queuing around the block. We had a cup of tea (or 'Rosie Lee', as Bestie always called it) before settling down for the interview. The conversation flowed, and we seemed to get on well. It was faultless, save for the fact that not a single word made its way onto tape. Try as I might, I couldn't get the bloody machine to work. 'Don't worry about it, we'll just have a chat anyway,' George had said, easing my embarrassment. In the end, Jimmy and I probably overstayed our welcome, carried away with this laid-back lifestyle in La-La Land. Later, the three of us strolled along the boardwalk, stopping outside Bestie's beachfront apartment to shoot the breeze and have a photograph taken with a beautiful blonde, one of George's many female 'friends' in LA. That snapshot is one of my most cherished possessions.

Meeting George and his buddy Bobby (who had won the Irish Cup with Glentoran in the '60s) was everything that we'd expected and more. It also gave me the opportunity to divulge that it wasn't just the Aztecs teammates who were born on 22 May. I was too. Over the years, it would become a standing joke between Bestie and me as we reflected, tongue-in-cheek, on the fact that 'two great wingers [sorry, Bobby] were born on the same day'. Before we left LA, there was one more treat in store for the Fullerton brothers. George and the Aztecs were scheduled to play Pelé and his New York Cosmos at the Los Angeles Coliseum. The crowd may have looked sparse inside that magnificent 120,000-capacity open-air arena (host to the 1932 Olympic Games), but it wasn't. Jimmy and I took our place alongside 44,000 short-sleeved spectators that day, all anxious to witness this clash of the titans. The match ended 2–2, neither Irishman nor Brazilian scoring, but no one went home disappointed. These were halcyon days for 'sawcur' in America, when the league was littered with top-class imported talent. That afternoon in LA's famous amphitheatre, players like Charlie Cooke, an FA Cup-winner with Chelsea, Phil Beal, formerly of Tottenham Hotspur, and ex-Welsh international centre-forward Ron Davies found themselves overshadowed by the brilliance of a 31-year-old Best and a 37-year-old Pelé.

I've always tried to remain impartial when it comes to that perennial pub debate about who was the greatest footballer. That said, I truly believe George Best was the finest footballer ever to emerge from the British Isles. His sublime talent also earns him a place in the game's holy trinity. The likes of Di Stefano, Puskás, Matthews, Platini and Cruyff are just some of those who can stake a claim, but in my opinion the top three greatest players ever to lace up a pair of boots were Pelé, Maradona and our own Georgie Best. In many ways, Diego Maradona was a throwback to Best and Pelé's prime, his instant control, devastating dribbles and venomous shooting illuminating a game that had long since given prominence to athleticism over ability. Raised in the slums of Buenos Aires, the fifth of eight children, Diego Armando Maradona would eventually see his career, and his life, spiral out of control to such an extent that scandal threatened to overshadow those dazzling skills. Bestie may have led a carefree childhood by comparison with that harsh existence amongst the shanty dwellings of Villa Fiorito, but he could certainly relate to the way controversy can cloud thinking and to the Argentinian's struggles with addiction. Kicking the ball was one thing, kicking the habit another. Neither man, it seems, possessed the capacity to cope with his fame.

It may seem like a contradiction in terms, but George Best

was a shy lad. Forget all the bright lights and bravado that characterised his days in Manchester; they merely masked a naturally introverted nature. Right from the start, he found things away from the mother he doted on too hard to handle, the 15-year-old Bestie scuttling back to Belfast with homesickness. Matt Busby persuaded him to return and shrewdly housed his prized asset with a lovable landlady, Mrs Fullaway. Those digs occasionally served as an oasis of calm in increasingly troubled waters. Otherwise, the only solace he could be sure of finding was in a bottle. Our friendship grew in no small part because I could empathise with George, at least to some degree. As a former footballer, whatever the standard I had played at, I could relate to the highs and lows of *his* game. I knew what it was like to score a penalty, how it felt to miss one. Perhaps, in a small way, I was also aware of the pitfalls and problems posed by life in the public eye. My experiences in that area were, however, small fry in comparison with George Best's goldfish-bowl existence. Bestie couldn't go anywhere. Stepping out of the front door or into a room was the cue for nudging and winking, for queues of autograph hunters, for an invasion of his privacy. George knew it came with the territory and would have signed till his fingers bled, but that didn't mean he always enjoyed it.

Only a few years ago, he made an appearance at the *Belfast Telegraph* Sports Awards. Within minutes of George taking a seat at his table, I was forced to make an announcement: 'Ladies and gentlemen, we're delighted that George Best and his charming wife, Alex, are here. Now, George is here, like the rest of us, to enjoy the evening. If you could please leave the autographs until after he's eaten.' The words had barely escaped my throat when people started making a beeline for Bestie once more, hands clasped around any available piece of paper. This wasn't Joe Public, either, but the great and the good of Northern Ireland sport and society. Whether he cultivated it or not, George Best possessed a charisma and charm that people found irresistible. From the moment he stepped off the plane from Lisbon, after United's 5–1 defeat of Benfica in the quarter-finals of the 1966 European Cup, with that sombrero perched on his raven locks, there was always someone who had 'El Beatle' in their sights.

It was at the height of the Troubles, and security was tight. I was driving George to catch a flight back to England when we were pulled over to an army checkpoint pitched on the periphery of Aldergrove Airport. 'What's the problem?' I asked the camouflaged soldier who knelt at my window. 'Oh, no problem,' he said, 'we just spotted George through our telescopic sights and wanted to meet him and get an autograph.' Then, looking at my passenger, the young English squaddie added, 'I hope that's all right, George, mate.' Countless times I've seen George Best attempt to melt into the surroundings, his face buried in a newspaper or one of the crossword puzzles he so enjoyed. Seldom did he succeed.

If Bestie bemoaned the fact that he was constantly in the spotlight, Joey Dunlop baulked at *any* sort of attention. Just how much he abhorred media intrusion was illustrated by his revelation to me at the King's Hall in 1977. Fresh from his first TT win, he and Davy Wood had been invited to appear at the annual Ideal Homes Exhibition. With camera in tow, I set course for what would be our first encounter since that spiky showdown at the motorcycle awards. Any fears I might have had that there would be fallout from our previous contretemps were soon allayed. Interview in the can, it was what Joey told me off camera that provided the real insight. I happened to ask, 'Joey, it must have been a great thrill to win an Isle of Man TT, I would say that's every road racer's big ambition.' Joey admitted he was delighted, not for himself but for John Rea, who had supported him. Then came a staggering confession. 'To tell you truth,' he went on, 'I was comin' doon the last lap and mae boards were telling mae I'm well in front and all I hae to do to win is no' fall off. As I turned onto the front [section of the course], I nearly switched her off. I knew they'd bae all standin' there when I crossed the line wae their cameras and microphones. And, Jackie, ye know what I'm like at the tawkin'.'

I found it incredible, still do, that he could have considered, even for a second, sacrificing that first TT win in order to avoid the likes of me. Of course, over the years, Joey won many more races and faced many more interviews. He improved as an interviewee, of that there's no doubt, but there was nothing to suggest he regarded that side the business as anything other than a necessary evil. Always content to let his racing do the talking for him, he was a winner who didn't care much for garlands and plaudits. That's not to say Joey was a soft touch when it came to money matters – far from it. He knew his own worth and fought his corner. Only it wasn't really *his* corner. His wife, Linda, once told me she believed Joey would have been more than happy with a wee house stuck somewhere up a mountain with no running water and a bike to tinker with. He was a man of simple pleasures, and certainly there were never any status symbols, no flash cars or designer labels. Money meant one thing to Joey: security for the family who accompanied him almost everywhere and to whom he was totally devoted. For Joseph, standing on the top step of the podium was maybe just a bit too much like showing off. Don't get me wrong, he did consider his successes something to celebrate; it's just that he preferred to do it back at the bar in Ballymoney.

It became a yearly ritual at Joey's Bar (formerly the Railway Tavern) to hang the same celebratory banner, with the previous year's total of TT wins scrawled out and a new figure inserted. Another custom was for Joey to bring the house down with his answer to talk of retirement. Our relationship may have got off to a sticky start, but my regular attendance at race meetings up and down the country convinced Joey I was genuine in my admiration for him and his sport. Gradually, he stopped viewing me as the wee footballer with the microphone. Eventually, I became the man he handed the microphone to. For four years in succession, I compèred those wonderful homecoming parties. Each time, I finished our formal chat by reminding Joey of his race wins and age, following this with the suggestion that maybe it was time to hang up the leathers. Each and every time, Joey gave the same answer, much to the delight of the bar's patrons: 'Jackie, you're a lot ouler than I am, and when you retire, I'll retire.' It was a particularly poignant moment for me when the Revd John Kirkpatrick, chaplain to Ireland's bikers, recounted the story of our verbal jousting during Joey's funeral service.

That Joey Dunlop shunned the spotlight most superstars crave was never better illustrated than on his beloved Isle of Man in 2000. Honda's new VTR SP1 superbike, with Joey on board, had made little impression at the North West 200 a few weeks before. Word was relayed to Honda that the King of the Roads was so unhappy with his new steed he was considering pulling out of the TT. It was a tactic, of that I've no doubt, and it worked a treat. Pulling out all the stops, the Japanese giant gave Joey the engine which Kiwi Aaron Slight was using in the World Superbike Championship. Specialised suspension mechanics were flown in; no stone was left unturned in their efforts to provide a competitive machine. With Honda's top brass having arrived to witness events unfold first-hand, the pressure on this 48-year-old father of five to win was immense. Add to the equation the pretender to his road-racing crown, Yorkshire's David Jefferies, and it was a high-speed showdown of epic proportions. Slight's bike proved itself to be a beast to handle around the island's roads, but a beast with real grunt.

It wasn't so much a case of riding it as guiding it, and there was no one better at exploiting that raw power than 'Yer Maun'. Joey steered his SP1 rocket-ship to a universally acclaimed win; hell, even the rival team's mechanics applauded as he took the chequered flag. At the moment of perhaps his greatest triumph, Joey again proved why the word 'humility' could have been invented for him. Declining the champagne offered by Honda's now ecstatic top brass, Joey chose instead to follow his own time-honoured post-race routine. Leathers rolled to his waist, lucky red T-shirt saturated in sweat, he sat in the back of his van drinking a mug of tea. Then it was off to the tent for a celebratory plastic cup of beer with his family and the rest of the boys from Ballymoney.

That George Best is an iconic figure is taken as read; Joey Dunlop's superstar status is not so widely acknowledged outside the bike fraternity. I recall, one evening on *BBC Newsline*, presenter Donna Traynor picking up on the fact that I'd mentioned Joey in the same breath as some more instantly recognisable celebrities. However, anyone who witnessed the buzz that greeted Joey when he made his way onto the grid, usually at least half an hour after everyone else, will know what I'm talking about. The moment he appeared, red lights came on and cameras clicked, everyone wanted a shot of the man with the number three and the trademark yellow helmet. Nowhere was he more revered than on the Emerald Isle, but we can easily forget that he had a truly global appeal. Bike fans in Holland, Germany, Belgium and the Baltic states, Australia, New Zealand and Japan all pay homage to Ulster's King of the Roads.

There's a tale (perhaps apocryphal, perhaps not) about one of Joey's trips to Australia, a favourite pre-season training ground in his later years. Blasting along the Australian highway on a borrowed bike, Joseph found himself pulled over by a police patrol. Before he had a chance to remove his lid, the cop says, 'And who do you think you are, Joey Dunlop?' Realising that was exactly who it was, the red-faced officer asked the five-times Formula One world champion to report to the local station. Thinking he was in trouble, Joey arrived to find a barbecue in full swing and a row of policemen looking for his signature on photos of him they'd downloaded off the Internet.

George and Joey were supremely gifted sportsmen with innate talent. To that they added self-belief (not arrogance) and a steely determination. Both men knew they were good, they just didn't feel the need to shout it from the rooftops. I remember one car journey with Bestie during which he was having a right go at the coach of his then club San Jose Earthquakes. George questioned why he was not making more of the talent at his disposal. 'We have three world-class players,' he insisted, 'Cubillas [a gifted ball-player from Peru], Gerd Müller [West Germany's muscular goal-scoring machine] and . . .' His voice trailed off. Bestie would never have said, didn't need to say, '. . . and of course there's me'. As well as the natural talent that coursed through their bodies, both men were able to draw on almost frightening reserves of resolve. Some of football's fiercest defenders made it their goal in life to kick lumps out of George, but on the odd occasions when they succeeded, he just picked himself up and tortured them some more.

Joey, too, didn't know when he was beaten. In 1989, he crashed heavily at Brands Hatch, leaving the circuit in an ambulance with a smashed right wrist and a shattered right leg that within hours would be held together by a rather crude-looking 18-inch steel pin. He was eventually transferred to Ballymoney's Route Hospital, and I went up to 'the Toon', as he called it, to interview him. The surgeon, Mr Robb, asked me to wait until they brought him down from the ward. 'Jackie, there's your man now,' he said, as they wheeled Joey in. I turned around, and there was this frail little man who looked about 80. I was about to ask 'Where?' when I realised it was Joseph. He looked awful. He was two and half stones lighter thanks to a week-long stay in an English hospital that didn't meet with his approval. I couldn't see this fragile figure ever racing again. Joey gave me the first interview since his crash and, inadvertently, another exclusive. Linda had given birth to the youngest of their five children, Joanne, only the night before. Despite the circumstances, the shot of Mum, Dad and baby girl was heart-warming.

I stayed on after the interview was over, and I later discovered it had meant a lot to Joey that I hadn't just grabbed the shots and run. As we talked, I asked him how difficult it would be to face racing again. Not difficult at all, he assured me. The way Joey saw it was that the accident had not been his fault; another rider (Belgian Stéphane Mertens) had misjudged his braking going into Paddock Hill Bend and taken them both down. It was just one of those things. Like his younger brother Robert, who suffered horrendous injuries in a crash on the Isle of Man in 1994, Joey faced the problem head-on. He swallowed his pride, trailing in behind riders more accustomed to being lapped. He ignored hurtful suggestions that he was living on past glories. He fought on until he proved the doubters wrong with a sensational superbike victory at the 1990 Ulster Grand Prix, ironically after a titanic tussle with his Rotary Norton-riding brother Robert.

Bestie, like Joey, was a winner. I've seen him spend an hour trying to kick a plastic ball through the legs of a chair, with just enough room for it to squeeze through. He liked setting himself a challenge, and that particular skill was to come in handy one Friday at Ormeau Leisure Centre. A few of us at UTV had a regular lunchtime five-a-side game going on, nothing too hot and heavy, just the chance to work up a sweat. George was in town to co-commentate with me the following day, so I asked him along. Bestie hung back as I walked into the dressing-room.

'All right, lads?' I said.

'No, not really,' one of the lads replied, 'we're a man short.'

'You're OK,' I assured them, 'I've got a lad here who wants to play. He plays a bit of football.'

To the dull thud of jaws hitting floor, in walked Bestie. For a bloke like Tony Axon, it was as if all his Christmases had come at once. An enthusiastic if limited footballer himself, he said to me afterwards, 'Jackie, I can't believe I played five-a-sides with George Best. I'll be dining out on this for the rest of my life.' It was a memorable experience all right, especially for UTV cameraman John Vennard. Unlike Tony, he was a more than decent footballer; he had played for crack Amateur League side Killyleagh in the Steel & Sons Cup final. Now, we all have to take turns in goal, and it happens to be John's shift. George is standing at the halfway line, ball at his toe. Suddenly, those hours threading that plastic ball through the eye of a needle come to the fore. With hardly any backlift, he fires in a shot, the ball spearing straight through John's legs into the back of the net. He was mortified, a situation not helped by me enquiring at the top of my voice, 'Did he just nutmeg you from the halfway line?' John laughs about it now – I think.

Laughter was never far away when you were in George or Joey's company. I spent some great evenings at the bungalow Joey rented during TT week. On one occasion, the flak was flying following the King's below-par showing, by his standards at least, in the 125cc race.

'That bike o' yours,' Joey said to Andy McMenemy, his 125 sponsor and one of the sport's great characters, '. . . useless!'

'No, Joey, it's you who's useless, you couldn't ride her,' Andy hit back in the blink of an eye.

But Joey wasn't finished. 'I could ride her,' he added, 'but, to tell you the truth, I felt like turning off the course, steering down to Douglas seafront and driving her into the sea.'

I saw my opening. 'Well, at least you wouldn't have been badly injured,' I suggested, with all the mock sincerity I could muster, 'not at the speed you'd have been doing.'

I might have had the last laugh on that occasion, but there was no doubting the king of the one-liners on a memorably wet night at Windsor. They were without question the most atrocious weather conditions I have ever worked under. George Best and I were perched on the roof of the stadium in a flimsy commentary box, with the wind and rain driving straight through the gap where the window had been. Admittedly, the lack of protection was my fault. Normally on a wet night at our national stadium, the elements blow down the pitch, not across. I was sure that by taking out the window I would alleviate the usual problem of steamed-up viewing. No commentator likes to work from just the monitor, so it seemed like a good idea at the time. Ten minutes into the match, and both of us are soaked. By half-time and our on-camera analysis, we look like a couple of drowned rats. My hair's matted to my head and my clothes are stained by rain. George has a far from flattering woolly hat on, and two more bobble hats are draped across our microphones like golf-club covers. As we talk on air, just out of shot, George Jones (himself a Manchester United and George Best fan) is frantically trying to hold the roof of our commentary box in place. It got so bad in the second half – during which both of us received electric shocks through our lip mikes – that we had to temporarily abandon our commentary (picked up by Mark Robson, who was presenting the programme back in a warm and dry studio), race downstairs to the parked satellite truck and continue there, following the game via the scanner's screens. Bestie was a real trouper, despite nearly getting a Don King hairdo. Even when Robbo introduced us laughing, he kept his powder dry. With the rain dripping off me, I looked at George and said, sarcastically, 'Ah, the glamour of television, eh, George?' Bestie just looked at the camera and, cool as you like, replied, 'Anyone got a gin 'n' tonic?' Stirred, but definitely not shaken.

Sadly for George, he was unable to stop at the odd G 'n' T. Anti-alcohol implants, health farms and bouts of cold turkey could not change the fact he was an alcoholic, a slave to the demon drink that distorted his normally mild-mannered disposition. I have to say, hand on heart, that I was never privy to the nasty side of George. I do admit there's considerable evidence that it existed, but I still find it hard to believe. That's because of the man I encountered countless times at awards, openings and annual dinners. Not only was he courteous and approachable but he also managed to keep, as they say in our neck of the woods, a civil tongue in his head. Anyone who has spent time in and around the game of football will be aware how free, shall we say, most people are with their language. Yet I can only recall one occasion, at an almost all-male function, when George Best used swear words, and they were only to help embellish his stories. I often watched news reports about his drunken rampages and found it well-nigh impossible to equate the shy man I knew with that snarling ill-mannered alter ego. I don't dispute every story – I wasn't born yesterday – but I do suspect George often suffered because of his reputation. We all know bad news sells better than good, and stories about Bestie always had news value.

I've seen with my own eyes how things can get blown out of proportion, not with Bestie, but another flawed genius, Alex Higgins. I was MC at a Higgy exhibition night in Coleraine, after which we decided to go out for a few quiet drinks. After stopping off briefly at the Lodge Hotel, where Alex and his girlfriend were staying, my mate Douglas Shek drove us all to the Strand Hotel in Portstewart. There was Alex, pint of Guinness in hand, trying not to spill a drop in Douglas's pristine Jaguar. The trouble started soon after we arrived. Alex was playing a one-armed bandit when this girl sidles up and begins chatting. There were no raised voices, no pushing or shoving, but clearly there had come a point in the conversation when Alex had asked the young lady to leave. She stormed off in a huff, and seconds later the bouncers arrived to evict Alex. That's when I intervened. I explained that if he had been out of line I would have most certainly have heard it from a few feet away. The problem was sorted out, but it did make me realise that notoriety is notoriously difficult to escape.

Booze can alter the mindset, making affable men angry. In George's case, it also made him unreliable. That said, in all the years I knew him, Bestie only ever let me down once. Sitting alongside me during a Best tribute night on UTV a few years back, Ian St John took great pleasure in recounting the story of the Bestie no-show. It was a bizarre tale of George, the golfer and a hole in the hedge. Bestie, the Saint and I were booked for a chat-show-style evening at a leisure centre in Belfast. Ian, who was staying with Linda and me, arrived early so we could grab 18 holes at the Raceview golf course in Ballymena. As we approached the fifth, my playing partner decided to get something off his chest. 'Are you sure George is coming?' he said. 'I've heard maybe he's having a few problems with the drink.' I was in the midst of telling the Saint there was no problem, in fact I was just getting to the bit about Bestie having never let me down, when a man suddenly appeared through the hedge. It was John McAleese, a top-class amateur player who happened to live on the edge of the course. He'd received a call from the office: Bestie's agent, Bill McMurdo, was looking for me. Poor Ian's still trying to come to terms with the fact that a bloke's just burst through the hedge like

David Bellamy as I disappear into the undergrowth. Using the telephone in John's house, I confirmed our worst fears. George wasn't coming. I returned to the fairway, where Ian was having a field day stating the bloody obvious. 'He's never let you down. Well, he has now.'

We did manage to secure a late replacement, with Maurice Johnston, the Bhoy who became a Gers man, coming to our rescue. Mo was a good get, but he wasn't Bestie, and the organisers of the evening knew it. 'Jackie, you're the Michael Parkinson,' one of them said, just before show time, 'go you out in front and tell them George isn't coming.' My response was just what you'd expect given my unique relationship with George and the fact that I'd arranged for him to take part in the first place. Peeking into the packed auditorium, I said, 'Go and tell them yourself!'

When George decided to go walkabout, there was little anyone could do. His first wife, Angie, found him in the midst of one bender shuffling along the street in the rain, soaked to the skin. It was at that point Angie knew that nothing she could say or do, not even the birth of their son, Calum, could curtail his excesses. Linda and I got to know Angie well. She has had her critics, the people who point to her autobiography and the fact that she didn't revert to her maiden name when the marriage ended, but to call Angie an opportunist is wide of the mark. It's only my opinion, based on personal experience, but I genuinely believe she loved him deeply, and still does. I met the second Mrs Best for the first time in Chelsea at George's 50th birthday bash. Maybe it was the age gap, but I never felt there was quite the same chemistry between Alex and George. That said, she was by his side for most of a difficult decade, during which the ravages of drink really kicked in. It can't have been easy.

You've got to hand it to George, he did have an eye for a beautiful woman. Blondes, brunettes, redheads, they all made a beeline for Bestie, and he, bless his cotton socks, did his best to ensure they weren't disappointed. With a track record of top totty that would be the envy of Casanova, you've just got to be interested to know who gets his vote as numero uno. I found out quite by accident as we were driving into Belfast city centre in 1982. George was giving me his critique of the gutter press and in particular their fascination with his love life. What angered him most was that these journalists having a go at him for going out with former Miss World Mary Stavin were, as he put it, 'overweight, sozzled by drink [which I thought was ironic coming from George] and probably married to pigs in lipstick'. Correct me if I'm wrong, but I think Bestie might have been hinting at a little jealousy there. The luminous Miss Stavin had visited Belfast the previous summer, accompanying George on his guest appearance for Glentoran against Manchester United. I had been on holiday with my family in Majorca and was disappointed to miss a match that I knew would mean so much to his dad, Dickie, a Glens fan. As we negotiated the traffic, Bestie filled me in on what I had missed, and he wasn't talking about the match. Mary Stavin, he confided, was the most beautiful woman he'd ever been with. Her eyes, her teeth, her figure, her skin – she was perfect. Stavin, quite clearly, was stunning. Of course, after the big build-up, this glowing description of his ideal woman, George smiled at me and said, 'As usual, I messed it up.'

It didn't sit easily with many people, myself included, when Bestie began abusing the new liver he received in a transplant in 2002. I can assure you, it didn't sit easily with George. To be honest, I always feared 'the wee man', as his international room-mate Pat Jennings christened him, might not be able to resist the temptation to get back on the grog following the transplant. I take no pleasure in having been proved right. Maybe George grew tired of fighting the cravings, maybe he knew he was on borrowed time and wanted to go out in a blaze of glory. Who knows? He certainly wasn't the sort of man to conform; he was a cavalier who chose to live life his way. Bestie wasn't perfect, but then he never claimed to be.

Joey, too, refused to play by other people's rules. With that natural reserve, rich County Antrim accent and aversion to attention, he was a PR man's nightmare. Even on TT presentation night, when he was invariably the centre of attention, he didn't like to be pestered. I recall standing with Terry Smyth and Joey's wife, Linda, at the annual bash in the Villa Marina in Douglas. A bloke from one of the television companies was hassling Yer Maun for an interview. He wouldn't take no for an answer. Clearly narked, Joseph looked over to where we were standing and barked, 'Linda, come on, we're going!' Linda, who'd long since learned how to read the signals, turned to us and joked, 'Look at the face on th'on! Somebody has taken the cream off his bun. I'd better go.' Joey Dunlop and George Best were capable of producing the sort of sporting virtuosity the rest of us can only dream about. But they also had flaws. In short, they were human, a fact that, sadly, became all too apparent.

On 2 July 2000, I was in the gym at Ross Park Hotel, near Kells, for my usual light Sunday workout. The owner's mother suddenly came over with a concerned look on her face. 'Jackie, there's some bad news. There's talk that Joey Dunlop has been badly injured in Estonia. In fact, the story is that he's been killed.' It couldn't be right. Not Joey. He'd told me in recent years that if he was ever in a fairing-to-fairing dice with a young rider or if someone near him seemed erratic, he'd back off. 'I'll no' be killing myself o'er the head o' it,' he'd say. I borrowed a mobile phone and called the office. A freelance reporter, who was completely unaware of my relationship with Joey, confirmed in the most matter-of-fact way that he was indeed dead. After surviving years of competing in the

Isle of Man TT and riding incredibly powerful superbikes, Joey died on the smallest, a 125cc bike. Although it was raining heavily and it's possible that he aquaplaned, no one is sure exactly what caused the crash. The circuit cut through a wooded area, and it appears that Joey hit a tree and fractured his neck.

I felt an overwhelming numbness take hold, a sensation which stayed with me for days. Somehow, Stephen Watson and I managed to bring out a tribute programme that evening. I'm still not sure how. We recorded a segment in which Stephen, who was also extremely close to Joey, interviewed me about my thoughts and recollections. Halfway through my first answer, I lost my train of thought and we had to start again. There were none of the usual nerves and adrenalin; it was as if I'd been anaesthetised. And so it continued. Monday, reported live from Joey's Bar for *BBC Newsline* – numb. Tuesday, reported live from the same place – still the same feeling. When I arrived home, I poured myself a large vodka, sat in the armchair and thought about Joey's parents, Willie and May, about Linda and the kids, and what they must be going through. Eventually, I began to leaf through the *Belfast Telegraph*, pausing to read John Laverty's sports column. John isn't a bike writer per se, but he is a damned good writer. His tribute to Joey contained some particularly poignant prose, and I finally broke down and cried.

I think it was that cathartic cry that helped me get through the funeral. For Stephen, it all proved too much. He was distraught as the coffin was brought out of the family home, and I put a hand on his shoulder as he, Terry Smyth and I waited for our turn as pallbearers. It was an incredible sight, with 50,000 mourners lining the Garryduff Road, and, just as the cortège moved off, there was a spontaneous outbreak of applause. It was something I'd never witnessed at a funeral, and my first reaction was to think how inappropriate it was.

Then, as the sound carried along on the country air, it suddenly became the most perfect accompaniment. The men, women and children with tears in their eyes were paying tribute to their hero in the most moving way. After the touching service was over, as the guests filed into the church hall next to Garryduff Presbyterian Church, I made my way to our television position for a live broadcast. As I surveyed the scene, it was we, the media, who suddenly seemed inappropriate. The church, the graveyard where Joey had just been interred, the floral tributes and wreaths were juxtaposed with cameras, cranes and satellite trucks. Here we were on one of the saddest days in Irish sport, scrabbling around to conduct interviews. And I was part of it. The scale of the event was staggering, the cross-section of people represented a testament to Joey's legend. I met a man from Cork who told me he would have travelled halfway around the world to be there. I met four lads who did. Expat bike fans domiciled in New York, they'd flown home together on Thursday to pay their respects. As I handed back to Donna in the studio, I concluded that I would 'never see a bigger funeral in my lifetime'. I was to be proved wrong.

The last time I saw Bestie was in March 2005, at Champneys, the Hampshire health farm where he was living at the time. It was shortly before his divorce from Alex was finalised, and he was in fine form. As we chatted in the complex's manicured gardens, I would never have believed that George would be fighting for his life in hospital just eight months later. During his last weeks, I deliberately avoided calling the Cromwell Hospital; it was clear the world and his mother would be trying to get in touch. I fervently believed, though, that Dickie, the family, Alex and George would know my thoughts were with them. Key to my friendship with George, and with Joey, was always the fact that I didn't suffocate them. When Yer Maun marched out to the TT grid with his scowling race face on, I gave him his space. Recognising when to step back, I never abused the privilege of spending time in their company. As a consequence, I was no more clued up during Bestie's final days than anyone else. Just like everybody else, I was glued to my television set for news. It was the picture published in the newspapers of a frail, jaundiced figure that exposed how forlorn my hopes of a recovery were; Denis Law's comments to camera about George being in a vegetative state that shattered them into a thousand pieces.

His passing was inevitable, yet that didn't lessen the blow for me when those three words, 'George Best dead', flashed across the screen just before lunchtime on Friday, 25 November 2005. The funeral was the biggest Northern Ireland has ever seen, and I remarked on air that the wee man would be looking down and smiling at the fact that he could still sell tickets. But then he always had pulling power. However, it wasn't just his enduring popularity that was on show that dark, dank Saturday; it was adulation, admiration for a sporting icon. He was a superstar who was also one of us. Bestie often said to me, 'I hope they forget the rubbish, and remember the football.' Wee man, they most certainly did.

I was heartened by the compliments I received following the George Best funeral programme on BBC Northern Ireland. It seemed I struck a different tone to others that day, my anecdotes helping to make the programme not just coverage of the funeral but also a celebration of his life. Quite a few people have also asked me how I managed to do it. Wasn't I supposed to be his mate? Shouldn't I have been too distraught to talk? Yes, it might seem strange that I wasn't overcome with emotion, especially when the cortège stopped 30 yards from our television point or when they lifted the coffin from the hearse. All I can say is that I haven't cried for George like I did for Joey. It's not that Bestie meant less to me; it's just that, as I write this, I still can't believe he's gone. I miss my friends, their warmth and humour, their humanity. What I wouldn't give to see Bestie in full flight with the ball glued to his boot and a glint in his eye, or the flash of Joey's yellow helmet as he and the Honda burn down Bray Hill. What I wouldn't give to be touched by their genius just one more time.

Chapter Nine

THE BIGGER PICTURE

This was my big chance. Impress in the next few minutes, and that transfer across the water, the opportunity to play in the big league, was there for the taking. As a footballer, I hadn't had what it takes to perform on the national stage; but as a broadcaster, I was confident I could cut it at the cutting edge. From the day and hour I joined the business, there had been glimpses of what was possible with talent, hard work and the right opening. Gordon Burns showed me the way. I'd taken the place he vacated at UTV; now, in December 1978, I was one good interview away from following him to Granada. I was far from the finished article after only six years in the business, but I had learned enough about my craft to seriously contemplate a cross-channel move. I was young, ambitious and anxious to mix it with the best. It was everything I had worked for. It was what I really wanted. I went to meet the interview panel determined to make my dream a reality.

Getting the job in Granada's sports news department would involve a game of two halves. It kicked off with an orthodox interview situation, a grilling that focused heavily on the news side, not my strongest suit. Part two – a screen test and mock studio interview with another applicant – was more my style. Now it was a question of whether my combination was the winning one. I didn't have long to wait for the answer. Before I had left the building, Paul Doherty called me over for a chat. The son of Peter Doherty, the legendary Northern Ireland player and manager, he was the station's top sports producer and would later become ITV's Head of Sport. Paul, who had given me some valuable tips beforehand, all but said that the job was mine. I couldn't wait to tell Linda. We had travelled over together to Manchester, spending the weekend in a pleasant little hotel on the outskirts of the city. George Best had arranged both the accommodation (the hotel owner was a mate of his) and tickets to see Andy Williams in the Apollo Theatre on the Sunday night. Linda, who was teaching at the time, flew back first thing Monday morning. I stayed on for the interview, catching a plane home later that evening. It had yet to be rubber-stamped, but I was within touching distance of achieving my ambition. It should have sparked celebrations in the Fullerton household, but instead it led to a sustained period of soul-searching. Wanting something is one thing, taking it another.

There was plenty to discuss. With a settled home life and three children under the age of eleven, there was more at stake than my aspirations as a broadcaster. Even when official word came that I was being offered the post, it did little to clear the muddied waters. One obvious stumbling block was the money. Granada were offering me less than I was currently on at UTV. Paul later informed me that the salary would have improved dramatically, that it was a case of getting my foot in the door, but at the time the issue did little to alleviate Linda's sense of unease. We continued to deliberate. One day we were going, the next we were staying put. If uncertainty characterised our thinking, that was hardly the case with one of my colleagues. Gloria Hunniford was adamant that I should take the job, something I relayed to Linda. Truth is, she was not best pleased with Gloria applying any more pressure – there was enough there already. Others, too, were in no doubt that I should pack my bags. Granada's net extended into the football strongholds of Manchester and Liverpool, something that attracted me to the job in the first place. Billy Bingham, who lived in Southport, felt sure that the North-west football fraternity would accept me with open arms.

Finally, just before Christmas, we decided to take the plunge. I prepared to make that life-changing phone call to Manchester, to set the wheels in motion. That was as close as I got. Everything was again put on hold. In what we were hoping would be our last conversation on the subject, Linda pointed out that Darren, our eldest boy, was taking his 11-plus. Acknowledging that a switch in schools could harm his progress, we discussed for the first time the idea of me commuting. The more I looked at the idea, the more I didn't like it. Sure, I would have enjoyed a few nights out with my colleagues in Manchester, but I envisaged spending most of my time sitting alone in digs, missing my family back in Ballymena. The planned 'big move' was beginning to unravel. Christmas, it has to be said, was not the ideal time to be making that sort of decision. Linda and I were becoming increasingly aware of how much family meant, how much of a wrench it would be to leave our parents. With the festive period further emphasising these issues and Granada needing an answer, I picked up the telephone and told Paul, 'Sorry, but I can't take you up on your offer.'

I don't blame anybody for me missing that particular boat. At the risk of sounding trite, it wasn't meant to be. It wasn't that the hurdles were insurmountable; Terry Smyth, for example, would later commute to the same Granada studios I had turned my back on. Maybe I just have to admit to myself that, although I wanted it, I didn't want it enough. Hindsight affords me the luxury of such analysis; back at the start of the '80s, I wasn't so philosophical. Giving up on my goal seemed to strip away all my motivation. In my mind, I was struggling to replace the dream I'd let slip away. There just didn't seem any point in showing what I could do if it wasn't actually going to lead anywhere. I can say without being melodramatic that it took two years for the gloom to lift.

Salvation came from an unlikely source, someone who had initially supported the move. It was Billy Bingham who alerted me to the possibility that I could have a fulfilling career closer to home. I knew Billy was keen for me to go to Granada, but when I informed him I was staying put for family reasons, he smiled at me and said, 'Well, Jeekie, there's nothing wrong with being a big fish in a small pond.' He was right. I had the chance to show my appreciation for Billy's counsel many years later. Billy Hamilton, Terry Neill and myself had accepted an invitation to take part in Bingie's annual golf day. Arriving the day before the event, we all met up for drinks and a spot of reminiscing. It was wee Billy who brought up the subject, and I took that as an opportunity to thank him for helping to open my eyes.

About six months after his own move to the mainland, Eamonn Holmes and I discussed life in the fast lane. 'You wouldn't have liked it over there,' he said, an indication, I presumed, that he felt my easygoing manner was not compatible with the cut-throat network game. 'You made the right decision,' he added. We've often joked about it since. With a feigned pained expression, I compare Eamonn's latest megabucks contract to my own. Then, sarcasm dripping from every syllable, I finish with: 'No, Eamonn, of course you're right. It was a great decision.'

Experience has taught me to take the rough with the smooth. A career in television is a roller-coaster ride. You can go from being flavour of the month to out of favour in the blink of an eye. You can be presenter of a television series one minute, minus a repeat commission the next. The secret is to not take yourself or the business too seriously. By embracing that ethos, I have learned to treat the peaks and troughs as sides of the same coin. That's why I was able to hack it when the axe fell on my *BBC Newsline* career in February 2004. It was certainly a bolt from the blue as far as I was concerned, but it wasn't the devastating blow to my ego that many people thought it must have been. Of course I was disappointed and, if I'm truthful, a little perplexed; but I didn't collapse in floods of tears or start sticking pins in voodoo dolls.

I think what helped was the fact that I was scheduled to travel to Estonia the day after the news dropped that I was getting the chop. It might have caused quite a stir in Broadcasting House and subsequently when it hit the newspapers, but it wasn't exactly the talk of Tallinn. Instead of mulling events over in my mind every minute of the day, I was able to focus on Northern Ireland's forthcoming friendly international. I also visited Joey Dunlop's memorial, stealing a few quiet moments after filming to reflect on more significant matters than my own problems. Tallinn wasn't a total escape, though, not in the age of the mobile phone. During the trip, I received numerous calls from people offering their support, including a shell-shocked Eamonn Holmes. He said, 'I don't understand why they're taking one of their top men off the screen. It's beyond me.'

He wasn't the only one trying to work it out. The newspapers inevitably got wind of the story, and Maureen Coleman from the *Belfast Telegraph* later phoned looking for confirmation of a tip-off she had received. 'Jackie, I'm led to believe you've been axed by *Newsline*?' I should have said 'No comment', but I didn't. 'That's a good word,' I said to Maureen. The word 'axe' appeared in the story's headline when it hit the newsstands on 26 March. It wasn't a case of biting the hand that feeds or betraying confidences; I knew that if Maureen had a sniff of the story, it was only a matter of time before it broke. Aside from corroborating the reporter's story, I didn't divulge any other information. I could have elaborated, put my side of things, but I don't believe in washing your dirty linen in public. That story, as well as a follow-up piece by Gail Walker published in the same paper, which was scathing about the Corporation's decision, caused quite a stir in the corridors of power at BBC Northern Ireland. I had been heartened by words of support from colleagues in Broadcasting House; but the genuine warmth shown to me by the man and woman in the street was overwhelming. The public's backing came in many different guises. One of the more amusing was Alan Simpson, MC at Coleraine Football Club's home matches. He appeared at the Showgrounds the following Saturday sporting a 'Save Our Jackie' T-shirt.

The truth is, I didn't actually want to be saved. I had become frustrated and a little disillusioned by the way sport seemed to be having to battle for its place within the framework of news, although in hindsight I can see that this was a time of transition. In an attempt to broaden our appeal we were treading a very difficult path. If you accept the premise that some viewers are alienated by sport, it can be easy to dumb down if you're not careful.

Thankfully, it appears that we have begun to get the balance just about right. Initially, I did, however, find it hard to break old habits and fully embrace the concept of treating a story in such a way as to engage those viewers with perhaps only a passing interest in sport. That's the balancing act I mentioned. You don't want to alienate the dyed-in-the-wool sports fan by insulting their intelligence. Likewise, you don't want the less fanatical folk reaching for their remotes. It was a difficult time for me personally, and, to be totally honest,

I began to realise that I wasn't enjoying my job as much. I found myself second-guessing the treatment of a story. Would it fit with this new newsroom approach?

It was one of the worst times in my career. Linda could see I wasn't happy. For the first time in 30 years, I didn't really want to get in my car and drive to work. I hadn't felt this bad since I was coming to terms with turning down the move to Granada. Saturday, at least, brought blessed relief. Commentating on the big local match of the day for the *Final Score* results programme was free from the pressure to conform to this new way of thinking. Now, it would have been easy to mistake my intransigence for a resistance to any alteration to the status quo. That wasn't the case. Satellite television and the plethora of new channels have raised the bar, particularly in terms of sport. Sky's treatment of football, for example, is light years ahead of the basic format of yesteryear. I have never been against change, but it took time for me to sort out in my own head that this new approach was for the better. It was against this backdrop that my final days as a *Newsline* presenter were played out.

Ironically, it was during this time that a supposedly old-school reporter with a soft edge to his journalism brought the programme two of the biggest local sports stories of the year. *Newsline* exclusively revealed that Sammy McIlroy was leaving the Northern Ireland job and that Glentoran were having the 12 points which had been deducted in a registration row dramatically reinstated. I even had the Glens' manager Roy Coyle sitting in the studio on the evening the story broke. I assume, however, that by then the noose was already tightening. Perhaps, my perceived failure to fully embrace the new way of thinking hastened my departure. I was eventually told that my *Newsline* presenting days were over, that I would not be an integral part of the revamped programme. My style didn't fit in with the 'new dynamic'.

The decision to call time on my *Newsline* career also had a knock-on effect on a relationship I've always held dear. For more than three decades, my wife has had to turn a blind eye to me talking to other women – men too, and kids. I suspect my rapport with the general public may never be quite as intense now that we're not communicating on a daily basis. Funny, really, that in the search for improved audience figures it should be deemed prudent to split us up. Only a few months before my axing, a member of senior management told me that a recent opinion poll had shown some interesting results. To the question, 'What does BBC Sport mean to you?' 77 per cent of people polled said, 'Jackie Fullerton.'

However, I can understand the pressures involved. Share of the audience is important, regardless of any spin to the contrary. For BBC Northern Ireland it means *Newsline* battling against *UTV Live* for the right to deliver the day's news. Over the years, the rival stations have adopted very different strategies. From its buzz phrase 'Your TV', it's clear what tack Ulster Television take. With presenters like Adrian Logan, Pamela Ballantine and Ivan Little, they play the local card, attempting to speak the same language as the man and woman in the street. The BBC's approach is different; because BBC Northern Ireland is a small cog in a very big machine, it has to be. Through no fault of the Corporation, however, that means BBC NI inherits positives and negatives. On the downside is the perception, thankfully now changing, that we patronise. I suppose it's a natural consequence of being good at something, but occasionally individuals can give off an air of superiority.

I saw it for myself many years ago when I was still at UTV. Robin Walsh, my old cricket buddy, had invited me to don the whites and guest for the BBC. Unfortunately, I was slightly late in arriving. When I eventually reached the dressing-room, I apologised, explaining that I had been held up editing some goals onto videotape. One of the Beeb team, who only a few months earlier had cocked up directing an international football match by cutting to the wrong camera at the wrong time, said sarcastically, 'Has someone round there learned to do that?' I looked at this bloke, whom I'd never met before (and who would eventually go on to become a friend), and answered, 'Yeah, and by the way, just you remember that I've seen some of the matches you've directed before you say too much.' That shut him up.

To be fair, sometimes the fault doesn't lie with the Beeb at all but with the public. Staff from other regions are often employed in Belfast, hence the range of accents you hear on reports. Many of these people are exceptional reporters in their field, yet they suffer because they don't have the local brogue. During the Troubles, in particular, I think many Ulster folk baulked at having people they viewed as outsiders telling them about their 'wee province' and its problems.

On the plus side, however, is the natural air of authority that the BBC has when it comes to the big event. I always felt the station had that edge myself. Even when I worked at UTV, I watched the FA Cup final on the BBC. Brian Moore might have been my commentator of choice for the rest of the season, but tradition told me – and thousands like me – that no one did 'big' like the Beeb. There's more recent evidence to back up this theory. BBC NI's live coverage of George Best's funeral attracted more than 300,000 viewers, a whopping 60 per cent audience share. It was also the programme that marked the return of the prodigal son. That's if you can still be called a prodigal son at 62.

I did so much work leading up to Bestie's funeral because people were aware of our friendship. Countless newspapers interviewed me, and I spoke to a seemingly endless stream of radio stations, including BBC Radio Five Live, BBC Radio Scotland and even one in Australia. A few days before the service at Stormont, I received a call on my mobile. It was my boss, sports editor Edward Smith. He explained that BBC Northern Ireland had decided to broadcast the funeral live. It was, however, to be a joint *BBC Newsline* and BBC Sport NI production. I knew what was coming. They wanted to know if I would work on the programme. It appeared to be the perfect moment to take my revenge for being sidelined as a *Newsline* presenter; after all, I was already going to the funeral at the invitation of the Best family. I chose to work. Why? That's easy. I did it for Bestie. If it sounds conceited, I'm sorry, but I wanted to ensure that someone said the right things about George. I wanted to tell people about the Bestie I knew, not parade out platitudes. I'm glad I did it, even after finding out from Castlereagh Borough Council on the day of the funeral that I would have been a pallbearer. I feel truly honoured to have been asked to perform that sad duty, but I'm glad I was able to play my part in a different way.

Events over the past few years, both personal and professional, have made me look at the bigger picture. There are certainly more important things in life than petty point-scoring and squabbles over television running orders. My departure from presenting sport on *BBC Newsline* is no longer an issue as far as I am concerned. However, that doesn't stop people asking me about it. Their assumption is that I remain a tortured soul seething with resentment. Nothing could be further from the truth. You see, I don't really do bitterness very well; it's not in my genes. That's not to say I'm being defeatist. Despite what has happened, my sangfroid remains intact. Hopefully, I will know when to walk away, I won't have to be pushed. Sadly, there's no escaping the passage of time. It just sort of creeps up on you. One day you find yourself looking in the mirror and not recognising the man staring back. But I'm not finished yet. I still love working for the Beeb. As I write this, I have just returned from reporting on

Northern Ireland's two-match tour of America for – yes, you've guessed it – *BBC Newsline.* If I ever need reminding that the passing years don't necessarily make you passé, I can check out national television. Parky and the two Desmonds, Lynam and O'Connor, are still proving that there's room for a good old 'un. Anyway, my very life depends on me continuing to work. Linda says if I was at home under her feet all day, she'd only end up killing me.

Chapter Ten

THE WONDER BHOY

It was one of the best goals I ever scored, a left-foot screamer into the top corner from 20 yards. Better still, it was at Windsor Park. Surely now, I thought, jogging back to the halfway line, we had finally seen off the challenge of the Whites and their whizz-kid. This, the second replay between Glenavon and Distillery in the 1971 Irish Cup, would indeed prove decisive. However, despite scoring in each of the two previous ties, and again on neutral territory, there would be no mention of the name Fullerton on the back pages. For my rocket at the Railway End was superseded by two from Distillery, and my spot in the spotlight stolen by a teenager. I'd read about this 18-year-old 'wonder boy', as the press christened him, and the impact he was having on the Irish League. All of us at Glenavon were aware he could, despite those tender years, hold the key to a place in the next round. That's why our hearts sank just a little when we scanned the team sheet before the opening tie at Mourneview Park. There, the boy in question having passed a late fitness test, was the name M. O'Neill.

Martin O'Neill lived up to the hype in all three games.

Deceptively powerful, with impeccable close control and vision, the Kilrea youngster plucked one perfectly weighted pass after another from his impressive box of tricks. Before the year was out, he would have made his Northern Ireland debut and signed on the dotted line for Nottingham Forest. Beating us that day at Windsor was just one more step for the 'wonder boy' en route to becoming a 'Bhoy wonder'.

Distillery, managed by Belfast Celtic legend Jimmy McAlinden, went on to win the Irish Cup that year, beating Derry City 3–0 in the final. Martin scored twice. It was glaringly obvious that young O'Neill was destined to follow his manager's example and head across the water. Jimmy McAlinden had played for Portsmouth, winning the FA Cup in 1939. Now his young charge was off to sample English football with Second Division Nottingham Forest. The breakthrough, though, didn't come immediately. Playing at Distillery alongside the likes of Roy McDonald, Peter Rafferty, Alan McCarroll, Derek Meldrum and George Lennox (with whom I eventually played in Crusaders' title-winning team) was a good grounding. But it would take the arrival in 1975 of a certain Mr Clough at Forest's City Ground to really kick-start his cross-channel career. Not that Cloughie made it easy for him – far from it.

Brian Clough and our Martin were a combustible combination. Cloughie liked his dressing-room to be subservient, but there was nothing submissive about his Irish midfielder. Martin might have given up his law studies at Queen's University to play full-time football, but he wasn't about to abandon the right to plead his case. In an interview I conducted with him a couple of years before he died, Cloughie offered an insight into their early association. He maintained that Martin was a regular visitor to his office, usually complaining about not being in the team and threatening to go back to Belfast to resume his degree. Finally, Clough had

had enough. In the middle of Martin's summing up, just as he was getting to the part about going back to Queen's and becoming a lawyer, Cloughie called his bluff. He opened his drawer, slammed a plane ticket on the desk and said, 'Well, there's your ticket, son, away you go.' According to Clough, that was the last he heard on the subject. Of course, Martin had a somewhat different recollection of events. 'That's a typical Brian Clough story, in that there isn't a grain of truth to it,' he told me. 'I never once mentioned university, or going home. If anything, he did.'

There may be more than a grain of truth in the O'Neill version. Brian Clough does appear to have had an issue with a player whose intellect was markedly higher than your average footballer's. Cloughie clearly preferred his players to be earthier and a little less cerebral. John Robertson, the cigarette-smoking, beer-drinking Scot who Cloughie himself once described as 'a little fat lad', could do no wrong. Martin, on the other hand, couldn't do right for doing wrong. 'You, O'Neill, what are you doing? You might have A levels and university training, but you can't play.' Nothing he did was quite good enough. Perhaps it was a classic piece of man-management on Clough's part, a sort of 'treat them mean, keep them keen' approach. 'I used to look over for a sign, maybe just one finger to acknowledge what I'd done,' Martin confessed. 'Mind you, it didn't pay to look too close, there might have been two fingers in the air instead of one.' Not all their spats, though, make for light-hearted reminiscences.

It was the morning of the 1979 European Cup final in Munich. Cloughie wandered over to speak to Martin and Archie Gemmill, both of whom had been taking part in a light workout to prove they were fully recovered from slight injuries. When he enquired as to their state of health, the manager was met with the sort of enthusiastic response you'd expect from two players desperate to return to the starting line-up. 'That's fine,' said Clough, 'you're both not playing.' Martin was devastated. Look closely at television pictures of the Nottingham Forest players and staff celebrating their 1–0 win over Swedish side Malmö, and Martin stands out. He's the one with a face like thunder. Even today, he can't bear to watch the header by Trevor Francis that clinched the trophy. For Martin knows that, as Robertson worked his magic down the left, he would have been making his move. As the hanging cross reached the far post, he would have been arriving. That was the area where he made his runs, that was his goal. Martin was inconsolable; even his wife, Geraldine, couldn't persuade him to take his place in the European Cup-winning squad photograph. It's something he now regrets. Still, his frustration was based on some fairly rational thinking. Martin, logically enough, assumed that a small club like Nottingham Forest could wait 500 years before reaching another European Cup final. How was he to know they'd be back the following year to retain the trophy with a 1–0 win over SV Hamburg and their star player Kevin Keegan?

It would be wrong, though, to paint a picture of manager and player constantly at loggerheads. That wasn't the case. They didn't always see eye to eye, but there was a mutual and abiding respect. Maybe they clashed not because of their differences but because they were actually alike. I mean, you both can't talk at once. Brian Clough was a whirling dervish of wisecracks and homespun wisdom, yet even he admitted Martin was 'the only man I know who talks more than I do'. But it wasn't just a shared gift of the gab that connected them. Clough confessed to me that, of all the players who had passed through his hands, Martin O'Neill was the one guy he was certain could make it as a manager. Maybe it's because, like Cloughie himself, he possessed a winning mentality, that innate ability to motivate and, of course, a certain charming eccentricity.

You can be sure of one thing: if Martin's comments had caused Cloughie any sleepless nights, O'Neill would not have spent a decade at the City Ground. Few questioned Brian's authority without paying the price. I was once told about a Forest player who went to see Clough on money matters. Apparently, the squad were unhappy about outstanding allowance money owed to them on an end-of-season trip abroad. Volunteers to confront Clough were decidedly thin on the ground, so they chose the club captain. Surely he could speak on their behalf without being beheaded. Cloughie certainly took note of his one-man deputation. The following season, he wasn't captain any more; in fact, he wasn't at the club at all.

Although, as a player, Martin O'Neill found his apparent failure to win Clough's approval infuriating, that sense of injustice passed. Both Martin and John Robertson thought the world of Cloughie, and they regularly went to see their old gaffer in his last few years. After all, they'd shared some memorable moments. Together, they had broken Liverpool's stranglehold on the First Division title, becoming champions in 1978 and finishing runners-up the following season. There were also two League Cup triumphs to celebrate, a feat Martin would later replicate as manager of Leicester City.

After serving his apprenticeship at the footballing outposts of Grantham Town and, briefly, Shepshed Charterhouse, Martin O'Neill's management career really took off when he steered non-league Wycombe Wanderers to the Vauxhall Conference title and into the Football League. Another step up the League ladder was enough to secure a more high-profile position, at one of his former clubs, Norwich City, but the stay was cut short when he resigned following a dispute with chairman Robert Chase over the availability of transfer funds. The Canaries' loss was Leicester City's gain, and it was at Filbert Street that Martin established a reputation for making the most of modest resources. Taking the Midlands outfit into the Premiership via the play-offs in his first season in charge, he then avoided the yo-yo effect that sees so many promoted sides returning from whence they came. But it wasn't just a case of survival. During his tenure, the Foxes were never out of the top half of the table, and they also bridged a 33-year gap without a major trophy by winning the League Cup in 1997. This time, the long-suffering supporters only had to wait three years before that particular piece of silverware returned to the Filbert Street trophy cabinet.

One of the central figures in Leicester City's success was a flame-haired midfielder from Lurgan. Neil Lennon's tenacious tackling and precise distribution proved invaluable for club and country. Martin acknowledged that contribution when he took him to Celtic. Following his compatriot to Scotland seemed like the logical thing for the player to do. It has certainly enhanced the Lennon medal collection, although at a price. Manager and player knew the move to Parkhead would not be popular with some sections of the Northern Ireland national team's support, the treatment meted out to a previous international and Celtic player, Anton Rogan, being a case in point. Both, though, must have been stunned by the level of sectarian hatred directed at Lennon, a campaign of abuse that culminated in death threats and the player's retirement from international football.

It would have been almost impossible for Martin O'Neill to refuse the Celtic manager's post when it was offered. Thousands of Leicester City fans holding 'Don't Go, Martin!' placards might have influenced his decision to decline the Leeds United job, but this was different. The name Glasgow Celtic Football Club has such resonance for Martin, the O'Neill family and his home town of Kilrea. Celtic was more than a mere football team; it was an expression of sporting tradition and cultural identity. 'Walk to Glasgow if that's what it takes,' was Martin's dad Leo's advice should his son ever have the chance to work at Parkhead. Neil Lennon, too, was a lifelong Hoops fan. There are some who would like to believe he pulled on the green-and-white shirt just to wind them up, but the truth is that Neil was being handed an opportunity to make his boyhood dream a reality. I attended his unveiling at Celtic. Martin, who was in particularly effervescent form that day, told the press, 'Well, he was a good player for me at Leicester, he'll do well for Celtic in Scottish football, and he'll help us win things. I don't want to put any pressure on him, but if he doesn't do well I'll kill him.' Martin's threat was tongue-in-cheek, but it was a tongue dripping with vitriol that phoned an altogether more sinister warning to the BBC on the eve of Northern Ireland's match against Cyprus in August 2002.

The hypocrisy, as well as the lunacy, would not have been lost on Martin. He captained his country at the World Cup finals in 1982, and, in gaining his 64 caps, he never once received abuse, sectarian or otherwise, from supporters. Even during Martin's time as Celtic manager, he appeared to be exempt. Before a Northern Ireland friendly with Germany, a group of former internationals were introduced to the Windsor Park crowd. There was no bigger cheer than the one that greeted Martin. At an event in honour of the 1982 squad held at the Culloden Hotel in North Down, there was no longer queue for autographs than the one wending its way to the Celtic manager's table. Hell, it didn't even seem to matter when I drew attention to the fact that Martin was the Bhoys boss. I was MC for the evening and, as per usual, Martin was giving me a bit of good-natured stick. The biggest laugh, though, followed my asking, 'By the way, what are you doing these days?'

Contrast that with the boos welcoming every touch of the ball by Neil Lennon during the match against Norway in March 2001; the picture of a hanged man daubed on a wall in Lurgan with the slogan 'Neil Lennon RIP'; and, finally, the brave patriot whose phone call warned that the midfielder would be killed if he played against Cyprus. That match would have seen Neil emulate his club manager, as his international boss, Sammy McIlroy, had selected him to skipper the side. I know there are some people who feel Neil should have ignored the threat, treated it as a crank call; that, by withdrawing from the match, he let the morons win. That's easy for them to say. Neil's family still lived in Lurgan, and the only way to guarantee their safety was to remove the source of the problem. So Neil Lennon retired from international football, and we lost an accomplished player. Some will say he wasn't that bothered anyway. Well, I beg to differ. I was in Miami's Orange Bowl in June 1994 when Neil Lennon made his international debut against Mexico. I have never seen anyone more excited or delighted about winning a cap for his country.

The Northern Ireland players were upset by Neil Lennon's departure, and that's as it should be. There's no place for religious division in sport, or in life. During Billy Bingham's reign, you could have said that the Northern Ireland football team was actually an oasis of tolerance in a desert of division. There were never any cliques, along religious lines or otherwise. I've seen at first hand what a close-knit lot they were. Bingie was, of course, always aware of Northern Ireland's tribal differences; he had to be during the '80s. I'm convinced that was part of his thinking when he chose Martin as skipper. Don't get me wrong, the Nottingham Forest man enjoyed the total respect of the players. He was the right man for the job. That said, I also think Billy knew the barriers he was helping to break down by appointing a Catholic as captain.

There's clearly a bond between Messrs O'Neill and Lennon, but not to the extent that the County Armagh man can expect preferential treatment. Neil told me that despite having worked under Martin at both Leicester City and Celtic he still remained on his guard. It's not a fit of teacup-throwing he feared, though; it was his manager's barbed wit. 'He's done a lot for my career,' Neil admitted, 'but even though I have to think he respects me as a player, I'm still wary of him whenever he walks into a room. I don't take liberties because he can quickly embarrass you with a one-liner.' I'm not sure anyone takes liberties with Martin. Certainly, I've learned over the years not to push too hard. When we were shooting the BBC Northern Ireland documentary *Man and Bhoy*, Martin always baulked at the idea of allowing us into the dressing-room. Getting a peek inside the inner sanctum would have been a real bonus for the programme, but when Martin made a decision, it was advisable not to question him. That's why we stood outside the dressing-room door after Celtic clinched the 2003–04 Scottish Premier League title at Kilmarnock, earwigging the celebrations taking place a few feet away. As we battled to resist the urge to burst through the door shouting 'Lights, camera, action!', a young lady appeared and enquired, 'Are you Jackie Fullerton? The boss wants you, he says you can come in.' The shots were great, although it did take some strategically placed towels to save the players' blushes and prevent our programme from receiving an X rating.

The champagne flowed, the craic was mighty, and our bonus material just kept on coming. Martin invited us back to Glasgow's Hilton Hotel later that evening for further festivities. We even sat at a table next to the players for the buffet. It didn't go unnoticed, and at one point Henrik Larsson ambled past. The Swedish striker looked over at me and joked, 'You back again?' I'd interviewed him a few weeks earlier, again thanks to Martin's personal intervention. John Robertson, O'Neill's former Forest teammate and assistant manager at Celtic, ferried us to the club's training complex about a mile from Parkhead. The other media guys were just leaving as we arrived, their allotted 15 minutes of training shots over. In a clandestine operation, we were sneaked past our broadcast colleagues and given free rein to train our camera on training. I happened to be wearing a long, black leather coat, and I could see the players glancing over, no doubt wondering why they were under scrutiny by the secret police. Martin, too, must have realised that our presence was having a mildly unsettling effect, and during a drinks break he put his players in the picture. 'Don't worry about this,' he said (referring to yours truly as 'this'), 'he's a friend of mine from back home. You won't be live on Bolivian TV.'

Later in the session, Martin came over to check everything was all right with us. I mentioned that he had previously said we might grab a word or two with Larsson. 'That'll be no problem,' he said, a bemused look spreading across his features, 'Henrik's a great lad, but he can be an odd bodie at times.' I had to laugh. Here was the media-savvy manager using a good old Ulster colloquialism. I suppose it was further proof that Martin O'Neill has never forgotten his roots. Larsson was charming, and extremely complimentary about his manager. You could say he had little choice; I mean, he couldn't really slag off the man who picked the team every week. However, there did seem to be a genuine respect and fondness. Even after he moved to Barcelona, when there was no barrier to an honest answer, Larsson has, in interview, expressed his admiration for Martin as both a football manager and a man-manager.

If Martin O'Neill is held in high esteem, it's no wonder. The balance of power was firmly with the blue half of Glasgow when John Barnes and Kenny Dalglish made way for O'Neill. Any silverware at all in that first season would have been an achievement, yet Martin managed to bag the lot. The Treble also proved to be the springboard for a first appearance in the group stage of the Champions League. The Lisbon Lions are the benchmark by which all Celtic sides are judged, but emulating the class of '67 had proved to be mission impossible. Both Old Firm teams found the transition from domestic football to an intensely competitive European scene a bridge too far. Then along came Martin, and suddenly Celtic was no longer a pushover, as victories over Continental aristocrats like Barcelona, Juventus and Liverpool emphasised. The club's real renaissance, though, came on that heady night in sultry Seville when Martin came within a hair's breadth of outfoxing 'the Special One', José Mourinho, in the 2003 UEFA Cup final against Porto. It was the Bhoys' first major European final for 31 years, and it rubber-stamped Martin's place in Celtic's Hall of Fame. The team was rejuvenated, reborn even, and Celtic's fans revelled in every success. They wanted more, they expected more, but it wouldn't come under Martin O'Neill.

On an emotional Wednesday, 25 May 2005, Martin announced his decision to step down as Celtic manager. His wife's continuing battle with cancer had to take precedence. '[Geraldine] has stood with me for all this length of time,' he said at the press conference, 'so I'll give her some time back.' Footie fans in the East End of Glasgow absorbed the shock, then sympathised and empathised with the man who had such a profound impact on their lives. The supporters' messages posted on the Internet told us all we needed to know about the relationship between them and their manager. 'I definitely shed a few tears today,' admitted one fan. 'The man who has brought me my happiest moments as a Celtic supporter has gone, and it's a pretty gut-wrenching day, to be honest.' Each tribute was personal and sincere. 'You may go, but you will never be forgotten. You have done us more than proud and there will be a place in my heart for you and your family always.' Many recognised his place in the pantheon of great Celtic managers: 'For returning Celtic to where they ought to be. For turning things around miraculously from where we were in 2000. For giving us back our pride (we never lost our faith). Martin, you are a Celtic legend.' Others struggled to express what they felt: 'Thanks for everything, Martin. I've tried five times now to write something else that conveys how I feel, but I just can't find the words.'

Martin is devoted to Geraldine and their daughters Aisling and Alana. You only need to see them together to realise that. The nomadic lifestyle that accompanies a career in football management doesn't always lend itself to domestic bliss, nor do the demands on your time and the unrelenting pressure. The pursuit of trophies, top jobs and financial rewards inevitably intrudes on family life, and it is impossible to get where Martin is today without making sacrifices. When his wife became ill, however, all attempts at balancing home and work became irrelevant. When Geraldine's condition worsened, Martin knew what had to be done. It wasn't a difficult decision to make, despite his love of the game and affinity with Glasgow Celtic, but it has required a seismic adjustment. We're talking here about a man who never sits still, whose grey matter demands constant exercise. I watched him on match days; never mind the animated touch-line antics, Martin's hyperactive long before he walks down the tunnel. Signing shirts, getting tickets sorted for friends, in the dressing-room, out again, checking that the crew and I were getting a cup of tea – he just didn't stop. To walk away from a job that pushed so many buttons, that provided the challenges his mind and body crave, cannot have been easy. For Martin, it was a case of priorities, and they had never been more clearly defined. 'What I do isn't very important in the grand scheme of things,' he told me. 'I'm not devaluing it, or being falsely modest, and it is important to me, to the club and to the fans that we achieve success. The real heroes of this world, though, are the doctors and surgeons. When you look at what they do, what I do pales into insignificance.'

I wasn't aware of Geraldine's cancer until we were nearing the end of filming for the documentary. Martin had given us fantastic access to himself, his staff and players, but we needed an insight from 'her indoors' to better understand the man. It was Dr Raymond White, a friend of Martin's since their schooldays at St Columb's in Derry, who eventually broke the bad news. For many years, Raymond has been his confidant, a benevolent figure he could turn to for advice and understanding. I'd spoken to Martin on a few occasions about interviewing Geraldine. He never mentioned her lymphoma; he just said she was shy (which she is). I had initially interviewed Mrs O'Neill after the League clincher at Kilmarnock. Now, at Martin's last match in charge of Celtic, the Scottish Cup final against Dundee United on 28 May 2005, Geraldine agreed to speak again. Trophy number seven safely secured, we returned to Parkhead, where Martin was rightly accorded a hero's welcome. With the celebrations in full swing, Raymond kindly brought Geraldine and the girls out to a quieter area for me to conduct the interview. It was the first time I had seen Mrs O'Neill since the day Celtic clinched the League at Kilmarnock. She looked pale and drawn. We hugged and I asked how she was. 'Never mind, how are you?' she replied, with reference to my own health problems. That's the measure of the lady. Despite her own troubles, she was thinking only of others.

Decency is at the core of the O'Neill family. But then, I've known Martin was a civil sort of bloke since the World Cup in '82. After the victory over Spain, Terry Smyth and I had arranged with Billy Bingham that Martin, as captain, would do a live interview for us at a Madrid television station. Technology wasn't what it is today, and our previous reports had had to be filmed, cut and then flown back on a daily basis. This one, though, was a case of pushing out the boat. Satellite time had been booked, and my chat with the victorious skipper would be bouncing straight back to Belfast. That was until Bingie had a change of heart, announcing after training that the deal was off. Terry blew a gasket. He and Billy went at it like cat and dog, the row threatening to boil over until Martin intervened. He told Billy there was no problem, that he was more than happy to do the interview. It speaks volumes about the man that he was willing to make an hour-long return journey into the centre of Madrid in a sauna-like taxi just to keep the peace.

I've seen many other examples of Martin's altruism, such as the trips he arranged to Parkhead for his old Distillery teammates. He also helped to pay some of the fares. It wasn't an act of charity; his generosity's not an act at all. He genuinely enjoys the lads' company, he loves to reminisce, and he has never become too big for his boots. It was one of the features that endeared Martin to my wife, Linda. She was completely taken by him from the first moment they met; she couldn't believe just how down to earth he was. But that's Martin, he doesn't have any real interest in celebrity. I mean, it took me about four years to get him to agree to the documentary. He said, 'Wait until I join a big club.' Then he joined Celtic. 'Wait until I win something major' was the next delaying tactic. Then he wins the Treble in his first season. Still, he wouldn't do it. 'Wait until I win something in Europe' was his final attempt at postponement. At that point, I said, 'Martin, I'll be retired and you'll be 100 before you win in Europe.' Nearly had egg on my face with that one, but at least Martin finally gave in. This was the result of my cajoling and the persistence (and charm) of the documentary's producer, Karen Bowen, whose mobile-phone bill ended up resembling the national debt of a Third World country. He may be in the public eye, but his private life remains just that. It's not that he's got something to hide. I was told that a tabloid journalist was going to follow Martin for a year to dig the dirt. He was forced to give up after three months because he couldn't find anything.

I like spending time with Martin; it's seldom dull when he's around. He has a wicked sense of humour and never misses an opportunity to have a jibe at Jackie. I recall a recent *Belfast Telegraph* Sports Awards where I was MC and Martin was announcing one of the category winners. As he opened the envelope, Martin pulled out his reading glasses. Then, looking in my direction, he peered over the top of the frames at the audience and declared, 'If Fullerton can wear them, then so can I.' You would think I might be offended that he used my surname, but even my wife commented on the affectionate tone used. It was typical Martin.

I don't know what the future holds for Martin O'Neill. At the time of writing, he is being tipped for virtually every high-profile job available. I fervently hope that Geraldine enjoys a full recovery, and that sometime soon we all get to see her hubby skipping along the touch-line again. Could it be Newcastle? Well, the Geordies would definitely take him to their hearts, and he could become a folk hero in another football-mad city. What about becoming Fergie's eventual successor at Old Trafford? Again, why not? He certainly has the self-belief that would be required to follow Sir Alex. Or maybe, as many would like to see, he'll become the new England manager. It makes me smile just to think about our Martin leading the English media on a merry dance.

Martin's press conferences were always entertaining, although I hadn't planned to be part of the amusement when I arrived in Glasgow near the end of his first season in charge. Celtic were closing in on a remarkable clean sweep of domestic honours, although there was still plenty of work to be done. As you can imagine, it was a particularly well-attended little gathering, with reporters, snappers and camera crews all jockeying for position. At one point in the proceedings, Martin looked in my direction and asked if I had a question. Now, I was a complete unknown to the assembled media, aside from one or two BBC Scotland lads, so there were a few furrowed brows as I launched into: 'Martin, it's hard to believe what's happened in your first season. You have to be thinking about the Treble?' Much to the delight of the journos, my query lit the blue touch-paper, or maybe that's green touch-paper at Parkhead. Martin tore strips off me. 'You come over here once, and the first time you're here you have the audacity to ask me a question like that.' He added something about not getting carried away, and then calmly moved on to the next question. The assembled hacks looked suitably smug as they reflected on the stunning stupidity of this Irish interloper. Of course, I knew Martin was only messing. After the formalities were over, he insisted I stay on for lunch. As we chatted, I asked again if he was eyeing the Treble. 'Of course I am,' Martin said with a cheeky grin. 'But do you think I'm going to tell those guys?'

Chapter Eleven

BIG RON'S CUP TIE

With more swagger than Jagger, and a smile etched across his permatanned face, Ron Atkinson led Manchester United out of the Wembley tunnel. Suited and booted, the sartorially elegant Big Ron revelled in moments like this. Alongside football's Champagne Charlie, looking understated by comparison, was Bob Paisley, in his ninth and final season as Liverpool boss. If fashion statements secured silverware, then the 1983 League Cup was already on its way back to Old Trafford. Suit by Jaeger, tie by José Piscador, jewellery from the model's own extensive collection, Big Ron was at his flashy and flamboyant best. How come I know quite so much about the Manchester United manager's outfit? Well that's because haute couture's House of Fullerton had accessorised his Wembley suit just a few hours earlier.

Terry Smyth and I met up with Ron at United's team hotel in the centre of London. We were shown up to Mr Atkinson's sumptuous suite, where the man himself was busy considering his choice of look for the big day. In front of him was a rack containing five, maybe six, spanking new suits, a freebie offering that Ron nonchalantly regarded as a perk of the job. He wasn't the only one, though, to enjoy such patronage, although mine was on a slightly smaller scale. A shop in Ballymena supplied me with ties to wear on television, and I had brought some samples with me to the Big Smoke. I showed them to Ron, drawing his attention to a particularly fetching striped number in navy and red, United's colours (or close enough, anyway). 'Spot on,' said Big Ron, as he pressed it against his chest. It certainly impressed my three United-supporting sons, Darren, Nicky and Gareth, that the manager wore their daddy's tie at Wembley. For me, too, it was a 'cup tie' to remember.

I'm surprised Ron didn't tell me to get knotted, for that little piece of Ballymena hanging around his neck didn't bring much luck. United lost 2–1 after extra time, and it was the retiring Bob Paisley who climbed the 39 steps to hold the cup aloft, his 13th major trophy. A few weeks later, the former Durham miner added number 14, the League title. Ron would discover, as McGuinness, O'Farrell, Docherty and Sexton had before him, that winning the latter was all that mattered at Old Trafford. The pressure to emulate Matt Busby's title triumphs in '65 and '67 may have been ever present, but it didn't stop Big Ron enjoying life at Old Trafford. From the moment he stepped through the doors in June 1981, it was as if to the manor born. 'Style with a smile' had been his motto since he started out in management with non-league Kettering Town a decade earlier. He replaced the small club's battered minibus with hired executive coaches, played Frank Sinatra tapes on away trips and dressed the players in pretentious club suits. It was like a dress-rehearsal for the day when he would manage a club of Manchester United's stature.

It wasn't just his extrovert personality that was tailor-made for Man U, though; his teams also played with the sort of attacking verve demanded by the Old Trafford faithful. After

Kettering came Cambridge and the Fourth Division title; a year later he was in charge at West Bromwich Albion. It was at West Brom that he really enhanced his reputation, building the Baggies into an exciting and highly effective unit. I first met Big Ron not long after he took over at The Hawthorns. He was taking his first tentative steps in broadcasting, co-commentating with London Weekend Television's Martin Tyler. However, it wasn't until four years later, at the World Cup finals in Spain, that we really got to know each other properly. He's a hard man to dislike. Ron's larger than life, loves a laugh, and, like someone else I know, fancies himself as a bit of a singer. Not surprisingly, we got on like a house on fire.

Terry Smyth and I became frequent fliers to Manchester during Ron's reign. It was a time when most players were still accessible, before agents and inflated salaries shot footballers into a different stratosphere from the man on the street. Still, this was Manchester United, and I found it hard to get my head around the access Ron was affording us. On one occasion, Terry and I were at Old Trafford for the Manchester derby. We were looking for presents in the club shop, a more modest affair than today's superstore. I was dithering as usual, and, when I walked out of the door, Terry was gazing down at me from the Manchester United team coach. So too were Robson, Whiteside, Moran, Muhren, Hughes and the rest of Ron's star-studded support cast.

'Come on, Jackie, hurry up and get on the bus,' shouted Big Ron. 'We're going for lunch.'

'We can't do that,' I said instinctively.

'Well, I'm the bloody manager, and I say it's all right,' Ron replied. 'Now get on the bus.'

So off to the Midland Hotel we went, taking our places alongside manager and players for the pre-match meal. It was like we were part of the team. Mind you, none of the team could eat like our Terry, not if they planned to put one foot in front of the other come three o'clock. Terence likes his food, it's fair to say, something that did not go unnoticed. Kevin Moran, who was sitting opposite, leaned over and said, 'You like the grub?'

'Yeah, yeah,' answered Terry, before taking up the offer of another player's leftover chicken. It was a touch surreal as we sat amongst the players watching *On the Ball* and *Football Focus*. I was just surprised Ron didn't go the whole hog and ask us to give the team talk as well.

The manager's office at Old Trafford had undergone something of a facelift since the departure of the comparatively austere Dave Sexton. It now boasted a sunbed and a much sunnier atmosphere. Ron liked nothing better than to have a few celebrities about the place, and, when we arrived back at the ground, Alex Higgins and comedian George Roper were waiting. As kick-off time approached, Ron stood up and, with his assistant Mick Brown, headed for the dressing-room. 'I'd better go and give the lads a gee-up,' he said, before turning around and placing his hand on Terry's shoulder. Then he leaned closer and said, 'By the way, who are we playing?' Terry took the bait hook, line and sinker, shooting back: 'Manchester City!' Big Ron looked at him as if to say, 'What do you take me for?' Then he grinned and walked out the door.

As it happened, Ron's half-time talk proved infinitely more profitable than that pre-match preamble. United found themselves two down to City at the interval, although, much to our amazement, there wasn't a word of dissension in the ranks. We were sitting in the seats which today are occupied by the United substitutes. In other words, we were close enough to the manager to hear any abuse hurled in his direction. It must be an English thing; I couldn't help thinking about the worldly words of advice that would be winging their way towards the dugout at Ballymena Showgrounds or The Oval if the home side were trailing by two in a derby. Maybe it was a show of faith, for Big Ron's boys came out a different side after the break to earn a draw.

After that League Cup final defeat in '83, Terry and I had tried to gatecrash the Liverpool celebrations. I made a particularly pathetic attempt at convincing my old mucker Graeme Souness that we were actually 'Pool fans', only to be greeted by a sarcastic 'Yeah'. He did have a destination in mind for the two bluffers, though. 'Go to Big Ron's party,' he suggested, code, I think, for 'Up yours!' We enjoyed more than a few glasses of vintage champers with Big Ron during his time at Old Trafford. The Manchester Reds may have lived in the shadow of the Merseyside variety when it came to League titles, but Ron did win two FA Cups, in 1983 and 1985. The latter victory and, more specifically, Norman Whiteside's glorious winning goal, epitomised the stylish, if not always successful, Atkinson ethos. Using Everton defender Pat van den Hauwe as a shield, Whiteside curled the ball inside Neville Southall's post to win it for a ten-man United.

The following season, Manchester United started like a house on fire, winning their first ten matches and remaining unbeaten after fifteen. Then came the slide. United finished a disappointing fourth. The party was almost over. North of Hadrian's Wall, a successor lay in wait. When the sack came on Thursday, 6 November 1986, United were nineteenth in the First Division, with just three wins from thirteen matches. Two days earlier, they had suffered a humiliating 4–1 loss to Southampton in a League Cup third-round replay. Ron had hit rock bottom. It was time to take it like a man, stub out the 'ceegar', clear the desk and head for pastures new. So Big Ron dealt with the disappointment of losing his job the only way he knew how. He hosted the mother of all farewell bashes at his house.

A reminder of where the new manager was born and bred replaced Ron's tanning bed. 'AH CUM FI GOVIN' were the words in capital letters above Alex Ferguson's desk at The Cliff, United's old training ground. To some observers, it might have looked as though Manchester United had deliberately scoured the four corners of the world to find a replacement as different to Ron as possible. Out went 10.30 training and the manager often rolling in late. In came 9.30 training with the boss already there and waiting. Out went the relaxed training sessions, sometimes nothing more than some shooting practice and a few drills. In came a tough training regime and serious attention to detail. It was bye-bye Mr Bojangles, hello Mr Tough Former Trade Unionist.

But it would be wrong to suggest that it was primarily Fergie's more disciplined approach that took him to Old Trafford. What closed the deal was his record. With a little help from a vibrant Dundee United, Alex and Aberdeen didn't just break the Old Firm monopoly, they shattered it. In 1983, the men from Tayside clinched the Scottish League by a solitary point, whilst the Dons retained the Scottish Cup and, rather more unexpectedly, won the European Cup-Winners' Cup. That extra-time victory over Real Madrid was only the third European trophy ever won by a Scottish club. The next season brought a domestic Double, League and Cup, for Aberdeen, followed in 1985 by a successful defence of their First Division title. Another Double, this time the Scottish Cup and Scottish League Cup, led to offers for Ferguson from his former club Rangers, as well as from Spurs and Arsenal south of the border. There was only one challenge Fergie really wanted, though: Manchester United. The changing of the guard at Old Trafford eventually took place in November '86.

A few months before that, I met both the outgoing manager and his soon-to-be successor at the World Cup in Mexico. With Ron, there as an ITV co-commentator and pundit, it was a case of renewing our acquaintance. With Alex, who had stepped into the breach as Scotland manager following Jock Stein's death, it was a brief introductory handshake before Northern Ireland's unofficial friendly with the Scots. That momentary pressing of the flesh was the extent of our familiarity. It would take a Glasgow Celtic legend and a hat-trick in South Africa to properly break the ice.

There's no doubting Alex Ferguson's affinity with Northern Ireland. His father, Alex Senior, worked for a spell in Harland and Wolff's Belfast yard, and, although the records don't appear to corroborate this, he apparently turned out alongside the great Peter Doherty at Glentoran. Alex Jnr played for Harmony Row Youth Club away against Ballymoney YM, at the Cricket Park (now the site of a supermarket). One of his opponents that day was a teenage Johnny McCurdy, later to be my Irish League nemesis. Coincidentally, Johnny's mother was originally from the Harmony Row area of Govan. Fergie was back in the summer of 1964, this time as a centre-forward with Dunfermline Athletic. Then 22, he scored in a 3–0 pre-season friendly win over Coleraine at the Showgrounds, although it wasn't the most memorable strike of his career. Victor Hunter parried a shot, and, as Alan Campbell attempted to clear the ball, it cannoned off Fergie into the net.

The autograph hunters may have given Alex a bye ball on that occasion, but three decades later they were queuing in their droves as the manager of Manchester United marched into Coleraine Showgrounds as guest of honour at the Milk Cup in 1994. His appearance, and that of his team, at the international youth tournament was down to one man – Bertie Peacock. 'The Little Ant', as he was dubbed after his all-action display in the 1958 World Cup, was one of Alex Ferguson's idols. Growing up in Govan, Fergie attended both Celtic and Rangers matches. His dad was a Celtic fan, he was a Rangers follower, and so it was a case of the best of both worlds. Bertie spent 11 seasons at Parkhead, becoming the first Protestant to skipper the Hoops. I was lucky enough to see wee Bertie in action myself as a wide-eyed and impressionable 13 year old. My Uncle Robert, who had his church ministry in Edinburgh at the time, split his leisure time between Hearts and Hibernian. When the Jambos reached the 1956 Scottish Cup final, he managed to get us tickets. Bertie played that day, although, if I'm honest, the reason I couldn't wait to get home had nothing to do with his prowess. I was just dying to tell the lads what it felt like being engulfed by that huge Hampden Park crowd of 134,000. I brought that game up in Sir Alex's company once, posing the question: 'Who was the Hearts left-winger who scored two of his side's goals in the 3–1 win?' In a flash, Fergie fired back the answer (Ian Crawford). He then named the other two scorers, not stopping until he'd rattled off both teams. He wasn't showing off, it was just a sign of his great knowledge of and passion for the game. Also abundantly clear was that Bertie Peacock had made a lasting impression.

The concerns Alex Ferguson expressed to Bertie were perfectly natural, and nothing he hadn't dealt with before as one of the founders of the Milk Cup competition. Some of the parents of players in the Man U youth team were understandably concerned about their sons' safety in a country still suffocated by sectarian strife. Sir Alex recounted his phone conversation with Bertie. 'I'm a football man, and you're a football man,' he said to the former Parkhead favourite. 'But we've got to think about the parents. They're worried about sending their kids to Northern Ireland.' Bertie, calm as you like, answered, 'Send them. It'll be OK.' That was it. If Bertie Peacock said it was OK, that was good enough for Fergie. The Milk Cup has since become an integral part of Manchester United's development of young players. Ryan Giggs took his Milk Cup bow in 1990. The following year, Fergie's fledglings, under the guidance of Nobby Stiles and Brian Kidd, won the Under-16 section of the tournament. The skipper that day was David Beckham, and the side also included Gary Neville, Paul Scholes, Nicky Butt and Keith Gillespie.

It was through Bertie that I got to know Sir Alex better. I think he filled Fergie in on my days in the Irish League. Despite its limitations, my football career gave me some credibility. What really clinched it, though, were those three goals I bagged for Boksburg against Bloemfontein. Bertie, Sir Alex and I were just shooting the breeze one afternoon and I happened to mention this hat-trick I'd scored in the Orange Free State. OK, so I happen to mention it quite often. What impressed Sir Alex most was that the opposing centre-half that day was a former star of Hibernian. 'You scored a hat-trick against Jackie Plenderleith?' he said, with what sounded to me like genuine respect.

I've come to realise over the past few years that Sir Alex Ferguson is a nice man. Now I am aware that 'nice' and 'Sir Alex Ferguson' are not often to be found in the same sentence, but I'm talking about the man, not the media image. I've always found Fergie to be approachable, affable and without the slightest hint of pretension. Mind you, I sure as hell wouldn't want to get on his wrong side. As he has proved on more than one occasion during his Old Trafford tenure, Fergie can strike the fear of God into the hardiest of souls. Cross 'The Govan-or' and it's usually curtains. Just ask Messrs Whiteside, McGrath, Ince and Stam if reputations count for anything with Fergie. That toughness, forged in his youth among the tenements of Govan, has helped make Alex one of the most successful football managers in history. However, it has not been allowed to eclipse an infinitely warmer side to his nature that emerges away from the cameras and bright lights. Witty, and with a disarming pride in and respect for his working-class roots, Fergie is as happy drinking out of a teacup as throwing one. He also cares about his family and friends, as I was to find out in the summer of 2004.

It was Milk Cup week, and things didn't feel quite the same; Bertie Peacock was in hospital for a hip operation. I phoned to pass on my best wishes, only to find the nurse on the other end of the line rather aloof. Within the hour, I found out the reason for her stand-offishness. My great mate Liam Beckett, who had played under Bertie at Coleraine, was the bearer of bad tidings. 'Jackie, terrible news,' he said. 'The wee man has just gone.' I thought of Bertie's wife, Ruby, his son, Russell, and the rest of the Peacock family. I also couldn't help thinking that Bertie had probably passed away at around the same time I was enquiring after him.

When I got over the initial shock, I decided to pick up the phone and called Fergie's secretary, Lynne. Manchester United were on a tour of the United States, and I asked her to pass on the news about Bertie. 'He would want to know,' I assured her. Next morning, around ten o'clock, my mobile rang. It was Sir Alex. 'It must be early with you?' I said. 'Yeah, five o'clock in the morning,' he replied. As it happened, he had been woken by the sound of a mobile-phone message coming through. He read it and phoned straight away from his Philadelphia hotel room. So to say he was deeply shocked by the news is an understatement. I asked if there was anything I could do at this end, perhaps flowers. 'No thanks, Jackie, Manchester United will take care of that.' I think it says a lot about Bertie Peacock that Sir Alex would call at five o'clock in the morning. I think it says a lot about Sir Alex.

Sir Alex and Big Ron have different takes on management, and on life, but they do share some common ground. Take their playing careers. Ronald Frederick Atkinson spent the vast majority of his career as a wing-half at Oxford United, earning the nickname 'The Tank' for his wholehearted approach to tackling. Fergie, too, took no prisoners during his time with

Queen's Park, St Johnstone, Dunfermline, Rangers, Falkirk and Ayr United, receiving the rather enlightening moniker 'Elbows' along the way. Both men also took time to hone their management skills before tackling the big boys. Ron busied himself with image makeovers at Kettering and Cambridge, whilst Fergie found his feet at East Stirlingshire and suffered the sack at St Mirren before challenging the Old Firm with Aberdeen. They have gone about the role of manager in very different ways, one with all the reserve of Liberace, the other with an inward-looking view of the outside world, a classic cultivation of an 'us against them' mentality. The goal, though, was the same. Ron and Fergie hate to lose, and each realised that in the Theatre of Dreams victory cannot come at the expense of entertainment. Football with flair has served them both well.

Of course, Sir Alex is 'the daddy' when it comes to trophies, but Big Ron has not done too badly himself. Two FA Cups at United, then League Cup glory with Sheffield Wednesday (whom he also saved from relegation) and Aston Villa (whom he took to the runners-up spot in the Premiership in '93). Both Wembley victories were over his former employer.

In the end, perhaps Ron's 'Mr Showbiz' image has actually done him a disservice. Many people see him not as a top-class former manager, but as the pundit who brought us such idiosyncratic terms as 'the lollipop' and 'early doors'. It has to be said he is prone to the odd commentary gaffe, known in the football fraternity as 'Ron-isms'. 'Beckenbauer has gambled all his eggs' is a favourite of mine. Or what about: 'There's a little triangle – five left-footed players.' Then there's the illuminating: 'Well, Clive, it's all about the two Ms – movement and positioning'; the mathematically challenged: 'He could have done a lot better there, but full marks to the lad'; and his wonderful description of our own Norman Whiteside: 'He's not only a good player, but he's spiteful in the nicest sense of the word.' It was all a bit of fun, at least until 21 April 2004.

Believing the microphone to be switched off after his commentary on a Champions League game between Chelsea and Monaco, Ron said, 'He [Marcel Desailly] is what is known in some schools as a f***ing lazy, thick n****r.' The microphone wasn't off. His racist comment was broadcast to countries in the Middle East, and the following day Big Ron resigned from ITV. Not long after, he parted company with *The Guardian* by mutual consent. Overnight the loveable buffoon had become the rabid racist. I was shocked, saddened and confused in equal measure by Ron's outburst. I'm not going to attempt to defend the indefensible, but I just cannot convince myself that the Ron Atkinson I know is some sort of heir to Oswald Mosley. After all, this is the man who signed Brendan Batson at West Bromwich Albion, completing, with Cyrille Regis and Laurie Cunningham, the triumvirate that became affectionately known at The Hawthorns as 'The Three Degrees'. It was the first time an English club had fielded three black players. This is the man who, as Manchester United manager, dragged me along to play five-a-sides at The Cliff one Sunday morning, a sweat session for ex-players that regularly included Stuart Pearson, Joe Royle and a certain Brendan Batson. And it was Ron who often fondly reminisced with me about the brilliance of Batson, Regis and Cunningham, and who was left totally devastated by Laurie's death following a tragic car accident in Spain. How do you equate these things with that bigoted remark about the Chelsea defender?

Big Ron has paid the penalty for speaking before he'd engaged his brain. After working for ITV at five World Cups and six European Championships, plus a host of Champions League matches, he opened his mouth without thinking one time too many. It's unlikely ever to happen to Sir Alex. Whereas Mr Atkinson was always regarded as quintessentially media-friendly, guaranteed to be ready with a quip or a one-liner, Mr Ferguson is a completely different animal altogether – especially if you work for the BBC. Fergie's relationship with the Beeb isn't so much frosty as frozen. He refuses to conduct any interviews with my national colleagues and is conspicuous by his absence on those *Match of the Day* post-match interviews. In March 2006, Sir Alex came over to Belfast to attend a tribute dinner to Bertie Peacock. He was in sparkling form that night, delighting the audience with his wit and candour as he chatted with me on stage. 'So you do talk to the BBC!' someone joked, reminding him of his running battle with the Corporation. Fergie just smiled and said, 'Only Jackie.' Aside from his usual humour, what emerged that night was a fierce determination to go out on a high. Fergie is aware he cannot go on for ever and that another Champions League crown is unlikely. One more Premiership title – well, that's a different matter. Sir Alex is currently learning to play the piano, something he tells me is therapeutic. I have a feeling that, for the time being at least, he does not intend devoting too much time to tinkling those ivories.

As for Big Ron's future, that's anyone's guess. It certainly didn't help his cause when he remarked at a Sheffield Wednesday function in January 2005: 'The Chinese people have the best contraception in the world – but I can't understand why there's so many of them because their women are so ugly.' On this occasion, he was probably the victim of a world gone PC-mad. It was a joke; one in poor taste, I'll admit, but it's hardly rampant racism. Given his recent record, though, it was particularly ill-judged. I hope Big Ron can get his life back on track; I genuinely believe he still has a lot to offer. I'll tell him that the next time we meet, just after I remind him he still has my tie.

Chapter Twelve

'WELCOME TO THE ZIPPER CLUB'

It was back, that strange squeezing sensation behind my chest. Not a pain as such, more a feeling of discomfort and the slightest hint this tourniquet might tighten. Still, I wasn't unduly worried. A quick spray of nitroglycerine under my tongue had done the trick before, if not instantly then within a couple of minutes. The first squirt was administered, but it failed to ease the pressure. The second was equally ineffective. Something was clearly wrong. My body was saturated in sweat, yet I felt cold. Anxiety took hold. 'Minimal trouble with a small artery behind your heart,' my doctor had said. 'All it needs is to put two stents in to widen the artery and let the blood flow.' Well, the stents (short steel tubes) were in and they weren't bloody working. It had all been so different just a few hours earlier, before that infernal heaviness once again infiltrated my chest. We'd chatted and laughed, Linda and I, enthusing about my release in three days' time. Now our plans were in disarray. Two more sprays of nitroglycerine failed to stabilise the situation, and, as medics buzzed around my hospital bed, I thought for the first time that I might actually die. I thought of Linda, our boys, my grandchildren, of not seeing them again. There was no sense of panic, no stomach for the fight, just a peculiar resignation.

The angina did eventually loosen its vice-like grip, but I still couldn't sleep. I was scared. Only as dawn approached did I finally slip into slumber. Later that morning, Linda arrived at the hospital, oblivious to the fact that I was now a pale shadow of the smiling man she had left the previous night. Before reaching my room, she ran into her Aunt Meta and Uncle Jim, the Galloways. They had been visiting a friend and were wondering, if it wasn't an imposition, whether they could call in with me. 'No, Jackie's great,' Linda assured them, 'you won't be bothering him.' The colour drained from my wife's face as she walked through the door. I looked like hell. My skin was a deathly pallor, I was badly in need of a shave and there was fear in my eyes. How Linda held it together, I'll never know. It must have been such a shock to see this decrepit, ghostly figure with wires and tubes protruding from chest and arm. It can't have been easy for Meta and Jim either, who had been led to believe I was doing just fine. Linda kept her emotions in check – she didn't want to upset me – but I found out weeks later that she broke down and cried within seconds of leaving the room.

The following day, I was taken back to theatre. There was an exploratory procedure, followed by a lengthy confab among doctors and consultants. As I lay waiting to hear the outcome of their deliberations, I felt oddly detached from everything going on around me. Finally, a registrar returned.

'We've got a problem,' he said. 'One of the stents has blocked.'

'What does that mean?' I asked.

He leaned over, gave my shoulder a paternal squeeze, and said, 'It means bypass surgery.'

With what must have seemed like the last word in bravado, I looked back and announced, 'Whatever it takes.'

Of course, this wasn't courage. I would have agreed to just about anything if it meant a return to normality. Ten minutes after they wheeled me back to my room, reality hit home. 'My God, bypass surgery,' I thought, without fully understanding what lay ahead. I knew enough, though, to realise it was serious. The word 'surgery' alone was enough to send shivers down the spine of a man who, in 61 years, had never succumbed to a scalpel. How could it have come to this?

Thursday, 9 September 2004 was when transitory twinges transformed themselves into a mild and lingering ache for the first time. It was the morning after Wales and Northern Ireland fought out a dramatic 2–2 draw in a World Cup qualifying match at the Millennium Stadium, and we were checking our bags in at Cardiff Airport. I wasn't feeling myself, although I didn't mention anything to my BBC Sport colleagues Brian Johnston, Joel Taggart, John O'Neill and Padraig Coyle. Then it started. There was no thumping pain, no agonising collapse on the airport-lounge floor, merely tightness. It lifted, and I didn't give it another thought. There were more pressing matters, after all. BBC Radio Ulster's *Talkback* programme wanted to discuss the match with me live over the phone. Twenty minutes after the angina attack, I was working again. The airport experience didn't play on my mind when I returned home, although I did make an appointment to see Dr Troughton at Antrim Hospital.

For the past few months, I had been taking medication for high blood pressure and I was becoming increasingly disillusioned with my lack of energy. At Galgorm Castle Golf Club, I needed the help of a buggy to complete 18 holes. It wasn't laziness on my part, just pure exhaustion. So, on the Monday, I drove to the hospital, convinced high blood pressure was the root cause of my problems. I was way off the mark. My blood pressure was fine, and, after an electrocardiogram

(ECG), my heart was also given a clean bill of health. Maybe I was fussing over nothing, maybe it was just age catching up with me. As I drove out of the hospital grounds, the time bomb was already ticking. Dr Troughton and I would see each other again a lot sooner than either of us expected.

I picked my grandson Jack up from Lifeboys (the junior version of the Boys' Brigade), returning home in time for the Champions League clash between Martin O'Neill's Celtic and Catalan giants Barcelona. Sitting in my usual seat in the kitchen, I logged the major moments of the match in preparation for cutting a *BBC Newsline* piece the following day. Without warning, the same discomfort I'd experienced in Wales returned. Only this time I was physically sick. Maybe I was in denial, but, despite the fact that all kinds of more serious issues were possible culprits, I chose to blame the nausea on the salmon I'd eaten for tea. Eventually, I made my way upstairs and lay down on the bed, but still the symptoms persisted. When I vomited again, Linda, who was becoming increasingly concerned, suggested I go to the hospital. I didn't argue, although I did take some persuading not to drive. In the end, I phoned our youngest lad, Gareth, who lived nearby. En route to Antrim, I dragged on a Benson & Hedges. 'That'll do you a lot of good,' Gareth chastised. It was my last cigarette.

My second ECG in just over 24 hours produced an altogether different reaction. The young female doctor who carried out the test wasn't specific, but she did tell me, 'There's something going on with your heart, we'd better keep you in.' I had a much clearer picture the following day. 'I didn't expect to see you so soon,' Dr Troughton said, before explaining my closing artery and the need for the stents. Obviously, it was not what I wanted to hear, but there was no great anxiety. Dr Troughton had a way of making it all sound so straightforward, and, to tell you the truth, my biggest bugbears were the week-long wait for the procedure and the fact that it involved a transfer to the Royal Victoria Hospital in Belfast. A boring seven days in hospital. How could they do that to me? It's amazing just how selfish you can become in situations like these. There were no more angina attacks until the Saturday evening. Two quick sprays zapped that particular episode, although it did have consequences.

The next morning, three days ahead of schedule, I was taken by ambulance to the Royal. There was nothing dramatic about the trip, quite the opposite. I laughed and joked with the doctor and nurse, even asking if it was possible to have the siren turned on. I'd watched enough movies to know a man should arrive theatrically at the hospital door. 'If there's a bit of traffic we might do that,' the doctor said, but, with the Westlink relatively free from cars, I had to be content with a more low-key arrival. Still, for a man about to have a stent procedure, I was remarkably upbeat. Was it down to Dr Troughton's reassuring words, or was I perhaps using humour as a defence mechanism? Either way, my mood was still good as I donned one of those not-so-flattering theatre gowns and listened to the modus operandi for stent insertion. Never mind that something would be fiddling about near my heart, I was more worried about them making an incision in my groin. 'I bet that hurts,' I thought to myself. I was conscious the entire time, flat on my back with a large plasma screen staring down at me. It was such a surreal experience, watching pictures from inside your own body and not having the first notion what they were revealing. Well, it didn't matter that I couldn't understand, as long as the blokes in the white coats did.

Everyone was happy, not least yours truly. The procedure appeared to be a resounding success, and, as each day passed, I became more and more like my old self. That was until that torturous Thursday evening when the stents stopped working, the blood stopped flowing as it should and no amount of spraying seemed to stop the rot. As I lay there contemplating my own mortality, I became overwhelmed by a sense of déjà vu. I couldn't escape the similarity between the events unfolding and the sudden death of my mother, just three years before. Mum had phoned from a shopping trip to town. She couldn't quite pinpoint the problem, but, like myself in Cardiff, felt that something wasn't quite right. I drove her to Antrim Hospital, where, with the help of medication, she made steady progress over the next four days. When my brother Jimmy and I left her around nine o'clock on the Wednesday, she was in great form. She was due to be discharged at the weekend, and we'd laughed and messed around, as only the Fullertons do, bantering her about having a wee hot toddy when she got back home. One hour later, I received a call from Jimmy's wife, Yvonne. She told me I needed to get up to the hospital urgently. As we raced towards Antrim, I said to Linda, 'I've a bad feeling about this.' I didn't even reach the ward before my worst fears were realised. As we approached Mum's room, a woman's wailing drowned out our clattering footsteps on the corridor floor. I recognised the voice. It was my sister, Mareen. In that split second, I knew wee Martha was gone. Three years on, and it was my health that was in freefall. Was I now going to leave my family to grieve over me? Was Mum's fate about to become my own?

I fell out with the world after my mum's death. I just couldn't cope. Maybe I felt that death's larcenous hand had robbed me of the chance to say goodbye. It wouldn't have lessened the pain, but it might have prevented the search for closure in the days, weeks and months that followed. If only we'd driven faster. If only we'd found a parking space a few seconds sooner. If only we'd run instead of walking. There's an Ulster saying, 'You've many things in life, but only one mother', and I wasn't ready to forgive myself for not being there at the end. Eventually, I did find a way to move on. Eight months after we buried Martha, my dad passed away. It hurt, but not in the same traumatic way. That's not because I loved my father any less, but because he'd been frail for quite some time. Mum's death was so unexpected; this time, I was prepared.

The evening before my mother's funeral, BBC Northern Ireland were scheduled to broadcast an episode of the sitcom *Give My Head Peace* that included a cameo appearance by George Best and me. The Corporation kindly asked if I wanted the programme to be pulled. I consulted the family, and we said thank you, but no. Martha wouldn't have wanted that. She'd have been laughing with the rest of us.

There was an ethereal quality to Windsor Park on 13 October 2004, at least from where I was standing. Silhouetted against the night sky by the floodlights' rays, my favourite place of work was like heaven on earth. As I gazed across the city from the hospital window, I would have given anything to be there. I watched the game on the ward television, trying not to get too overexcited as we surrendered a lead then fought back for a last-gasp draw with Austria. Before the match, I'd phoned my young colleague Joel Taggart, who, in my absence, was making his live television debut as a commentator. He's a likeable lad, and I wished him well. Still, I had to remind myself he was only keeping the seat warm. In 12 days' time, I would go under the knife for bypass surgery; then I'd be back.

It's the waiting that does it. Every day you're up with the birds, sitting there all bright-eyed and bushy-tailed with bugger all to do. You can only read so many newspapers, thumb so many magazines, and even watching the small-screen television installed in my room made my eyes tire easily. I paced the corridors of Wards C and D until I knew every nook and cranny, pressed my nose against the windows to watch labourers at work in the hospital grounds. I was never a great fan of manual labour, but I would happily have changed places with any of those lads. Saturday was the worst. I watched blokes heading into a boozer beyond the Grosvenor Road, imagined they'd be having a lunchtime pint before placing a bet and heading to the game. I missed my own match-day routine. I missed commentating, the craic and an evening meal with Linda at our favourite Chinese restaurant in Galgorm.

I longed to get out, and yet it wasn't so long ago I didn't want to leave. One of my biggest fears on hearing that I needed bypass surgery was the delay. Taking into account my recent track record with angina, I was reluctant to return home. Ballymena to Antrim isn't far, but what if I took a turn and didn't make it in time? Linda, too, was in a quandary. Sure, she wanted her hubby home, but she wouldn't be able to relax for a second in case the tightness returned. Fortunately, my brother-in-law David (Russell) is a professor of medicine in Oslo. He phoned my registrar, Professor Jennifer Adgey, a very impressive and assured lady, and between them they came to the conclusion that I should stay put. It would be nearly five weeks before I was wheeled to theatre, hence my battle with boredom. With all that time on my hands, and the lingering fear of the unknown, it's remarkable that I didn't seek solace in a packet of 20.

I'm not one of these born-again non-smokers who preach with an evangelist's zeal against the evil weed. Maybe it's wrong to say this in our ultra-health-conscious world, but I liked to smoke. I'd still like to. Even as I write this book, 18 months fag-free, I can't say to you that I will never light up again. In latter years, I became infuriated by Bestie's inability to beat the booze. Everyone was telling him the damage it was causing, and yet he continued to break the seal. Maybe I understand his dilemma better now. Drinkers and smokers who choose to quit are a different breed from those forced to abandon their addiction. Quite simply, I didn't want to stop smoking. I knew I had to, but it takes more than some carefully chosen words and a few leaflets extolling the virtues of nicotine patches to kick the habit. Now, it has to be said that I was relatively free from cravings during the seven weeks I spent in hospital. Maybe it was the medication that took the edge off things, but I never once found myself lingering outside a smoking room or sneaking outside for a quick puff. However, I still pulled out all the stops when Professor Adgey told me I had to quit. 'What about cigars or a pipe?' I enquired, despite the fact that I dislike both. Plain speaking was clearly needed, so the Prof barked out, 'I said no smoking!' I felt like a naughty schoolkid caught having a cig around the back of the bike shed.

They warned me that I might get tearful at some stage. I laughed. Me, the former footballer who'd run the gauntlet of the Irish League's granny-kicking full-backs? Then it happened; a chance change in my surroundings was enough to turn on the waterworks. I was moved to an isolation room ready for my impending surgery. It was bigger than my previous room and brighter, too, but the move shook me from my comfort zone. I cried liked a baby. I just couldn't help myself. That was only the beginning. My generation has generally regarded heart problems, of whatever variety, as a signal that your life is over. I worried about ever working again, and, before I knew it, tears were streaming down my face. I blubbed three times a day for a week, on two occasions I even cried myself to sleep. I thought about my mum and dad, how distraught they would have been at my predicament, and sobbed uncontrollably. Maybe I hadn't properly grieved, maybe I'd worked too hard at blocking out the pain. All these suppressed emotions bubbled to the surface, and there wasn't a damn thing I could do about it.

As D-day approached, opportunities to put the operation to the back of my mind rapidly decreased. The day before my operation, I was asked to shave not just my face but also my entire body. I shivered as I stood in front of that full-length mirror shaving my chest. 'Tomorrow they'll be cutting this skin,' I thought, 'and not just that, they'll be opening my breastbone to get at my heart.'

Earlier in the week, two nurses had called with a book illustrating the bypass procedure. 'Do I really want to see this?' I asked. Of course, the hospital is legally bound to make you fully aware of what lies ahead, so they flicked open the book. I wasn't too bad, but Linda, normally such a strong lady, looked as though she was about to faint. There was a picture of a man propped up in bed with breathing tubes down his throat and a huge rectangular plaster running down his chest. If ever there was a time to contemplate the seriousness of bypass surgery, it was now. But, instead of worrying about my chest being sliced open, I thought to myself, 'I'll bet it really hurts when they pull that plaster off.' A visit from my registrar didn't help bolster my confidence either. If someone was to tell you that their friend had a 98 per cent chance of surviving heart bypass surgery, it might seem like pretty decent odds. When it's you, that 2 per cent failure rate comes sharply into focus. It's a wonder people don't just bolt out of bed and leg it. Thankfully, I had Linda and my family to allay my fears, plus two unexpected visitors, both of whom helped me through that unforgiving weekend.

Billy Anderson is a well-known local businessman and was then president of Ballymena United. We'd known each other for years, and I was delighted he took the time to call on me. Billy, though, brought with him more than an old pal's kind words. Just 18 months previously, he had undergone the same triple bypass surgery I was facing. Listening to Billy telling me how much he'd worried before the operation and how two days after the op he berated himself for being so uptight was just what the doctor ordered. I also had a visit from Gerry Brammeld, a former striker with Drogheda United and Coleraine. For a while, I forgot my woes as we reminisced about players and games. Then, as he was about to leave, Gerry reached into his pocket. 'I know you're a Protestant,' he said, 'but would you take this?' He handed me a little prayer, which I kept at my bedside for the rest of my stay in hospital. I'll never forget what Billy and Gerry did for me. They have no idea how much it meant.

Billy was right. A couple of days after my operation, I was already feeling better than I had done for months. In layman's terms, the surgeons had made an incision through my breastbone and spread open my chest to expose the heart, which was then stopped with a mild electric shock. Veins taken from my leg were used to create three bypasses, allowing the blood to circulate without travelling through the blocked arteries. Then my heart was restarted with another shock. To tell you the truth, I didn't much care for the finer details. All I knew was that the men in the surgical masks had handed me a second chance. As the days passed, I grew stronger, physically and mentally. It's not just the body that feels the strain, your confidence and self-belief suffer too, so it was a great help that I was inundated with letters and cards, from family, colleagues at work, friends and complete strangers.

On one occasion, Linda arrived bedside with a huge grin on her face. She shoved a mobile phone to my ear, and I listened to Sir Alex Ferguson wishing me a speedy recovery and promising to phone again. 'He's just being nice,' Linda said, but a couple of days later, just as she was putting her items through the till at the local Co-op, Fergie did indeed call back. Poor Linda had to make excuses to the girl, and to Sir Alex, as she made her way outside. Well, you can't really say in the middle of a supermarket in Dunclug, 'Could you just look after those things for a moment? Sir Alex Ferguson's on the line.'

Jimmy Nesbitt also called the hospital. I sent my son Nicky to chat to him on the reception phone and to ask if he wouldn't mind ringing me on the line next to my bed. As I picked up the receiver, I put on my best smoothie broadcasting voice and said, 'League leaders Linfield . . .', as Jimmy, an ardent Coleraine fan, associated me with that opening gambit. 'Never mind all that nonsense,' Jimmy replied, with all the feigned irritation he could muster, 'this call is costing me 47 p a minute, so I hope you're short of breath.' I've watched Jimmy's career with great interest over the past few years. I knew his father, James, and particularly his Uncle Bertie, a journalist and great local character. Quick-witted, fun to be with – I can see a lot of Uncle Bertie in Jimmy.

I have bundles of card and letters at home, and each one means the world to me. There is a particular piece of correspondence, though, that is a little special. Not because it came from a former president of the United States, but because of the empathy shown. William Jefferson Clinton had bypass surgery a month before me, and I recall reading an article in which he described his feelings on the subject. Directing the comment to his wife Hillary, who was getting upset, he said, 'Now you steady on, darling, we dodged a bullet here and survived.' His letter, signed by hand, echoed many of my hopes and fears.

I, too, feel as though I've 'dodged a bullet', never more so than when I think of Cormac McAnallen, the young Tyrone Gaelic football star I had the privilege of meeting on a number of occasions, or John McCall, the teenage Royal School, Armagh, rugby player. They were cut down suddenly by heart problems at a young age, and yet an old codger like me is given a second chance.

Getting out of hospital was only the beginning. Once

the initial euphoria had evaporated, there was a period of readjustment, a time in which it was necessary to resist the natural urge to become a recluse. Post-operative depression is common, and I had no qualms about taking medication to lift the gloom. I also heeded the advice I'd received before leaving the Royal. Get out of the house as soon and as often as you can, the doctors told me, and, two weeks after lying on that operating table, I accompanied Linda on a shopping trip to Sainsbury's. It's easy to wallow in self-pity, to worry that everyone will think you're an old broken man. Getting out, answering enquiries from shoppers about my health, experiencing the public's warmth, it all helped to ensure my mental health kept pace with my physical recovery. I told so many people I felt fine that it gradually dawned on me I might actually be telling the truth.

I took it one day at a time, one step at a time, not least in my ongoing battle with cigarettes. Being back home was far more difficult in that respect than my stay in hospital had been. When I sat in the armchair, my first reaction was to look for the cigarettes that had always been perched within easy reach. After every meal, first thing in the morning, last thing at night – kicking the habit meant breaking old habits. It's funny, but my heart condition had shattered an illusion about smoking. For years, I fooled myself into thinking there was a trade-off, that the time I'd spent playing football and exercising my heart had somehow built up brownie points for my retirement from the game. Smoking 25 to 30 cigarettes a day was OK, because I'd earned it. Since leaving hospital, I've been asked to recount my post-operative experiences in a series of meetings with doctors, nurses and other medical staff. I said that there was a weakness in the system when it came to the treatment of smokers. The prevailing attitude was still patronising and lacked understanding of how hard it is to break that nicotine addiction. I think those medics who've never smoked fail to fully appreciate why we lit up in the first place. Bottom line, we bloody well enjoy it. Ask anyone who has stopped smoking and they'll tell you, if there were no ill effects, most of them would start again at a click of your fingers. My own father gave up for seven years, but near the end of his life smoking was one of the few pleasures he had left. I haven't had a cigarette for more than 18 months now, but I don't consider myself to be a non-smoker. I'm just a smoker who chooses not to smoke.

Life goes on. The sooner you realise that, the sooner things can return to some semblance of normality. Some aspects of life, of course, will never be the same. My work in television used to mean everything to me; now I see it for what it is. I'm well aware that it's a cliché, but if you don't have your health, you have nothing. Time with Linda, the boys, my grandchildren Erin and Jack – that's what is truly important to me now. I still love my work; don't get me wrong. From the moment I walked out of the hospital, I was aiming at a return to the small screen.

I eased myself back in with an Irish Cup commentary at The Oval, knowing full well that it was only a few minutes' edited highlights on our *Final Score* results programme. It was the live post-match interview with my old mate Roy Coyle that made my palms a little sweaty. I had already checked with the doctors if a burst of adrenalin might have adverse side effects, but was assured that the medication would keep things in check. As I stood there waiting for the presenter, Mark Sidebottom, to hand over to me from the studio, I had this horrible feeling, just for a split second, that I wouldn't be able to remember Coyler's name. As things turned out, it was like riding the proverbial bike. I settled into that familiar patter, proving that I was ready for the next stage in my recovery. Commentary at a wet and windy Windsor Park friendly between Northern Ireland and Canada upped the ante. However, the real goal was – and had been since the whole roller-coaster ride began – to be at Old Trafford to commentate on our World Cup qualifier with Sven's England. Now I had to make the Theatre of Dreams more than just a pipe dream.

I pass the road leading to Antrim Hospital on the way to work. Each time, I say a prayer. I think of Mum, how she died, and how the doctors and nurses cared for me in *my* hour of need. The angina attacks, the surgery – they're not always in the forefront of my mind. Most of the time I just go on living. In truth, it's easy to forget, easy to look ahead not back. Occasionally, though, I can't escape the past. Sometimes when I'm brushing my teeth in the morning, I catch a glimpse of the serrated scar that cuts my chest in half. It's almost like delayed shock as you stand and wonder, 'My God, did that really happen to me?' It did, and that scar marks a rite of passage. It's why Graeme Souness started his goodwill message to me with five meaningful words: 'Welcome to the Zipper Club!'

Chapter Thirteen

'WE'RE NOT BRAZIL, WE'RE NORTHERN IRELAND'

With just 15 minutes and counting until kick-off at Old Trafford, it was time to take a final look at my notes and focus the mind. Oblivious to the noise inside the stadium, and the camera crew that had been following me since breakfast, I readied myself, steadied myself, for the job at hand. Then a lone voice broke through my fragile cocoon of concentration. 'Jackie, listen to the Tannoy,' it implored. It was a member of John Daly's team, which was charting my comeback for the BBC NI series *A Day in the Life of* . . . Seconds later, the PA system sparked into life. 'A special welcome today after his recovery from serious illness,' said the stadium announcer in a melodious Mancunian burr, 'please welcome Jackie Fullerton from BBC Northern Ireland Sport.' Applause rang out around the ground. Then, from the stand away to my right, the one housing nearly 7,000 'Norn Iron' fans, came the Green and White Army's personal greeting. 'One Jackie Fullerton, there's only one Jackie Fullerton,' sang the boys in a gesture of support I won't easily forget. They'd chanted my name before – usually, it has to be said, with a whimsical request for a song. It was a connection with the supporters I had come to love. It was our joke. But this was different. Manchester was an important milestone in my recovery from surgery, and I like to think the fans knew that too. Instinctively, I stood up and waved back, appreciative of their warmth and understanding. In that instant, before a ball had been kicked, I had achieved my goal.

I could barely hear myself speak as the gladiators emerged from the tunnel into the Old Trafford arena. Ticker tape fell like confetti and flags thrashed from side to side as a sea of faces focused on the international footballers of England and Northern Ireland. For the two sets of supporters busily cranking up the volume, there were contrasting expectations. Those in red, white and blue were banking on an easy three points, with perhaps a bit of shooting practice for Rooney and the boys thrown in for good measure. If you were wearing green, it was as much about the occasion as the result. Win, lose or draw, they would back their team to the hilt. They had waited for a match like this for nearly two decades, having last played England in 1987. It might have been just another game for the English, but this was like a World Cup final for us. Players, supporters and the media had been looking forward to this fixture from the moment Sven's *galacticos* were drawn in the same group.

In the weeks leading up to the match on 26 March 2005, there was a growing sense of anticipation. It proved infectious. I visited the mainland on a couple of occasions during the build-up, a useful dry run for my first lengthy spell away from Linda since getting out of hospital. A few precious hours were spent with Bestie in Hampshire, the very last time I was to see 'the wee man'. Then, in a hectic two-day shoot in London, I spoke to Terry Neill and Pat Jennings. As we stood beneath the famous Highbury clock, Terry and I reminisced about his winner against England back in '72. The following afternoon at White Hart Lane, big Pat Jennings took me back to that heady night when he performed heroics between the sticks to secure our place in Mexico. With each passing day, I found myself getting more and more excited. I hadn't looked forward to a match this much since the days of Billy Bingham.

At Northern Ireland's team headquarters, the picturesque Mottram Hall, a rambling old hotel in the Cheshire countryside, there was a tangible link with the past. Bingie's legacy to Lawrie Sanchez was the perfect propaganda tool with which to wind up a jingoistic English press: the British Home Championship trophy. Having been transported with the kit on the short flight from Belfast, this stunning piece of silverware enjoyed pride of place during Northern Ireland's press conference. It was a little reminder that on our day, back in the day, we weren't half bad. The mood around Mottram Hall was fairly relaxed, or at least it appeared to be so. If the lads were nervous, and given our position in the world rankings there was every reason to be, they showed little sign of it.

I was also doing my best to make it look like just another day at the office. In truth, it felt like the first day at the office. I hadn't been living in fear since the operation, but I did occasionally wonder if this was all too much, too soon. Only natural, I suppose. What my brittle confidence needed was a boost. Cue Keith Gillespie, the Bangor lad I jokingly refer to as 'my fourth son'. Keith is an honorary life member of the Likeable Rogues Club. He's also become a good friend over the years, and I've been delighted by his resurgence as an international player under the new regime. There's always plenty of banter when Keith's around, and not even heart surgery is off limits when it comes to a bit of mickey-taking. The first time I saw the players at Mottram Hall, one of them shouted, 'Hey, Jackie, I hear you've got a new heart.' Quick as a flash, Gillespie pipes up, 'Sure, he never had a heart to start with, wasn't he a winger?' That repartee worked wonders for me.

But it wasn't just the players who welcomed me back. The Northern Ireland manager also more than played his part. Lawrie Sanchez can sometimes appear rather aloof, but he has been anything but cold with me. Back in October 2004, on the night of the World Cup qualifier with Austria, his kind words helped lift my mood. Someone had left a copy of the match programme for me, and, as I sat on the hospital bed, I flicked through the pages. In the manager's notes, Lawrie had written that the players were saddened to hear of my illness and that everyone hoped I'd be back at the mike for the England game. It was easy to feel forgotten; that article was a timely reminder to me that I wasn't. Then, just before Christmas, Lawrie phoned to check how I was getting on. At Mottram Hall, he was particularly affable, even stopping for a quick chat on camera (again for the Daly doc) before boarding the coach to the stadium. It's hard to overstress the importance, when you're still carrying so much emotional baggage after such a lengthy spell on the sidelines, when your self-belief has been sapped, of feeling part of things again.

I travelled to Old Trafford with Terry Smyth. It was good to have him by my side. We'd been through so many scrapes together over the years, and I felt more confident, more secure, when his support was close at hand. As we approached the stadium, the adrenalin began to course through my body. It was unmistakably match day. The Northern Ireland fans were out in force already, shouting and singing, creating a carnival atmosphere. With their good humour and almost childlike fervour, they were clearly intent on making this an occasion to remember, not just for themselves, but for anyone who crossed their path.

I found myself smiling. This was a day for them, for lads

like Roy 'Skin' Martin, Hugo the taxi driver and Joe English, with whom I worked at STC in Monkstown. These guys and the hundreds just like them are the real supporters. They had paid their dues during previous campaigns on foreign fields; they deserved a day out in the sun. As fully fledged foot-soldiers in the Green and White Army, they had proved themselves ready and willing to follow their team to the ends of the earth. Near-Arctic conditions in Armenia – they were there. Football outposts like Albania and Azerbaijan – count them in. Our Skin even managed to get himself invited to a wedding in the Ukraine. I shouldn't have been surprised; I mean, this bloke has more front than Jordan. In Armenia, he suddenly appeared inside our commentary box, having somehow blagged his way into our ice-cold cement bunker. It's bloody well hard enough to get into these places with a media pass at times, yet there's Skin nodding his head in approval as Alan McDonald offers analysis on some replayed action. Roy's always up for a laugh, as he proved about 20 minutes before that 1–0 defeat in Yerevan in 2003. It was my last opportunity to nip to the little boys' room before kick-off, and, as I was leaving, I ran into Skin and the lads. Mr Martin and I were chatting away when one of his mates hollered, 'Hey, Skin, don't you be tapping Jackie for money.' Roy told them – colourfully, shall we say – just where to get off. Then the two of us hatched a plan. As we stepped towards his mates, Skin stuck his hand out like Oliver. Then, in a loud voice, I said, 'Skin, that's all the change I have,' whilst at the same time dropping a few worthless local coins into his palm. We could hardly keep our faces straight as the boys went bananas at their mate the cheeky beggar.

It's not hard to see why the larger-than-life Skin proved such a hit with the Ukrainians. About three hours before we were due to depart for the ground in Donetsk, the BBC television and radio commentary teams joined forces for a bite of lunch. As we strolled the few hundred yards to the restaurant, I began to wonder if the Ukrainians were actually vying for the title of most romantic nation on the planet. I witnessed at least four weddings taking place during our short walk; perhaps it was just a popular time of year for nuptials? Roy and the boys happened to be downing a few pre-match drinkies themselves in the same establishment, and they were regaling the locals with tales about yours truly. The next thing I know, two Ukrainian footie fans amble over and introduce themselves. Good English-speakers, they chatted away until my food was about to be served. At that point, Skin calls Joel Taggart over. 'Is Jackie all right with that pair of boys?' he enquired. My young colleague assured him there was no problem. 'That's all right, then,' said Roy, nodding, 'but if there's any trouble, you give me the nod and we'll sort it out for Jackie.' Not just my mate, but my minder as well.

As it transpired, the only thing Skin had to sort out was a suit. He and a couple of mates had been drinking with the locals the previous evening, and they stumbled upon a stag night. When the Belfast crew eventually parted company with their new Eastern European friends, they did so with an invite to the following day's wedding. Sure enough, just three-quarters of an hour before kick-off, I looked out of my commentary position and there's Skin, dressed to kill, marching along the bottom of the grandstand. 'I see you got to the wedding,' I shouted. Skin looked up, smiled and pulled his jacket lapel towards me as if to say, 'I scrub up OK, don't I?' Someone told me the ever-resourceful Mr Martin had actually borrowed the jacket, shirt and tie from one of the Northern Ireland players.

I was to be thankful for Skin's ingenuity on the plane home from the Ukraine. The IFA had decreed that our charter flight be a model of temperance. It was a pity because there were a few of us on board who liked to unwind with a couple of shorts. Somehow, in an airport that was spartan at best, Roy had secreted about his person a litre bottle of vodka. It was soon mixed with Diet Coke to produce a not-so-soft drink and passed to those in need. Several players, who shall remain nameless, made full use of this mobile optic. I was also more than happy to indulge when asked, with a nod and a wink, 'Would you like a wee drink of Diet Coke, Jackie?' Maybe I shouldn't have been quite so keen, for I'm sure that industrial strength concoction could have been used to strip paint off walls.

I can only try to imagine how it feels for a footballer to walk down the Old Trafford tunnel at five to three, into that imposing arena. I found it exhilarating enough, and there wasn't a fan in the place. That's not to say I was alone with my thoughts. In addition to the countless television personnel, stewards and security men busying themselves ahead of the match, I was shadowed every step of the way by a cameraman, soundman and presenter. As John Daly and I walked around the pitch perimeter, there was an inescapable buzz about the place. There were a few familiar faces in the vicinity, too. Iain Dowie and Graeme Le Saux stopped to shake my hand. 'How are you, wee man?' big Iain asked. 'I'm great,' I replied, 'I only have three months to live, but I'm great.' As the words tumbled out of my mouth, I worried what Linda might think of my flippancy. Fortunately, when it was broadcast in the documentary, she, like Iain, saw the funny side. At lunch in the media centre, Alan Green of Five Live came over and gave me a big hug. There were others too, from the print media, who passed on their best regards.

Eventually, after talking half of Old Trafford through my surgical procedure, it was time to make my way to our commentary position, a sort of eagle's nest that dangles from the roof of the grandstand. Fortunately, I'd worked at Old Trafford before, commentating on a League Cup tie, otherwise that bird's-eye view might have caused me a flutter or two. It was an area we shared with the Sky Television team, Martin Tyler and Trevor Francis, plus national BBC's main man, John Motson. I chatted with Martin, like myself a long-time member of the Brian Moore fan club, and exchanged pleasantries and a few stats with Motty. He had heard on the grapevine that I'd been ill, but was surprised to learn of the bypass. 'My word, and you're here,' he said, adding that I looked as though I'd lost weight. 'About a stone and a half,' I informed him, 'although I don't recommend the diet.' John Motson is what I call a 'football man'. It's his great passion in life, and, although he's been at the top of his game for many years, he remains dedicated to his work.

Armed with a couple of insightful anecdotes courtesy of Motty, I returned to my seat alongside my co-commentator for BBC Northern Ireland, Alan McDonald. I was there when big Alan made his international debut against Romania in 1985, although we had first met many years before. His brother Roy was Crusaders' reserve goalkeeper during our Gibson Cup-winning season. Alan was a regular on the Seaview terraces as a kid – he even admits to having once asked me for an autograph. There had been occasions in the past few months when I had questioned whether it was all worth it. In the morning, when I was, to use a good old Ulster colloquialism, hoking around for my daily quota of tablets, it was as if what was left of my vitality was draining away. Now, amongst friends and with kick-off minutes away, I felt like a kid again.

I wouldn't get a job on a travelling circus with my powers of prophecy, but I did call the game pretty well that afternoon. During the half-time interval, John Daly interviewed me about the opening 45 minutes. I said that Lawrie's lads had done really well, but we'd given so much in the first half. Chasing a slick England side around Old Trafford is bound to take its toll, and, when you tire, you inevitably make mistakes.

Mistakes lead to goals. I finished by saying that, on the first-half showing, we wouldn't deserve to be on the receiving end of a 4–0 beating.

There was no disgrace in defeat that day. Once Tony Capaldi's misplaced pass on the edge of the box gifted Joe Cole the opening goal at the beginning of the second half, Beckham and the boys looked a more than useful outfit. It was disappointing, yes, but this was the millionaires' club versus a team that included lower-division players and one, Chris Baird, who was making the transition from reserve-team football at Southampton. As the teams made their way towards the tunnel, I wrapped up my commentary: 'So the final scoreline – a very disappointing scoreline at Old Trafford in this World Cup qualifier – England 4, Northern Ireland 0. Back to the studio in Belfast.' The second I finished speaking, my body quivered with a pulse of pure euphoria. I turned to Alan and then noticed the documentary camera was still rolling. Looking straight down the lens, I smiled and gave the thumbs-up. It was one of the best moments in my life. I will always look back on 26 March 2005 as a great day. Who was to know that there was an even greater one to come?

A small group of fans, most of them parents with children, formed an unofficial guard of honour at the entrance to Windsor Park. They were there to welcome England's superstars. Some, like the wee girl with the Real Madrid number-23 shirt, could barely contain their excitement. It's not every day in Belfast that you get the chance to glimpse a global football phenomenon. And a glimpse was all it would be. Aside from a strictly observed 15-minute window of opportunity for television crews and photographers, this was a behind-closed-doors training session for Sven's squad. Suddenly, the coach came into view. Stewards on the gates sprang into action, and, with military precision, the England team swept inside the stadium. The little lass with the replica shirt saw nothing more than a few silhouettes through heavily tinted windows. It was the same at the Culloden Hotel, England's team headquarters. The Football Association not only secured the entire hotel for the duration of their stay (heaven forbid the players would have to fraternise with local guests), they also turned the grounds into a no-go area. When the team first arrived in the province, they were driven to within feet of the Culloden's front door. A few profile shots of players getting off the coach and scurrying inside was all we had to report on television; they had already avoided detection at the airport by leaving through a side exit. As for the fans, standing a few hundred yards further back, it must have been a huge disappointment. Not a single player waved or even looked in their direction. Were they worried we might put them under some sort of spell?

The Football Association's paranoia extended to questioning my BBC colleague Stephen Watson, who was using the hotel as a backdrop for his live presentation into *Newsline*. They were concerned that we might be training our camera at the window in an effort to get shots of Becks and the boys. Stopping short of laying a minefield on the front lawns, the FA threw a ring of steel around their camp. The entire operation was a perfect example of how today's millionaire footballers are becoming dangerously removed from the fans. I don't blame the players, more the authorities. Sure, the squad should be allowed privacy in which to prepare for the match, but, as we were not expected to pose much of a threat, why was no consideration given to a little positive PR? Ironically, it was the man with the brand, David Beckham, who proved to be most in touch with the fans.

Two stories sum up the English attitude to the game. One relates to a supporter, the other a journalist. A BBC crew in the centre of Belfast interviewed a group of English fans. It was good-natured stuff, with the reporter finishing by asking for a prediction. 'Result? Well, you're looking at four or five nil,' said one of the lads, before adding, 'At half-time.' It didn't cross his mind that this would be anything other than a cakewalk in Windsor Park. History was on his side, to be fair. Northern Ireland had only beaten England twice, home or away, since 1927. In fact, the year Lindbergh flew solo across the Atlantic was also the last time we reached the dizzy heights of a win over England at Windsor. To be brutally frank, I would have taken a 2–0 defeat before kick-off. On the evidence of the first match in Manchester, this English side looked capable of slamming a sizeable score past us on our own patch. I was also convinced that the days of us springing a massive upset were long gone. During Bingham's reign, when Spain and West Germany were turned over, we had a team made up mainly of players in the top flight and a fortress for a home stadium. Now the team was drawn from clubs like Crewe Alexandra, Plymouth Argyle, Hull City and Motherwell.

So, we've established that an English win was on the cards. All it needed was a little humility. Let's be honest, though, that's not a trait in plentiful supply when it comes to English football, especially amongst the xenophobic elements of their press. My son Darren was in the packed press-box when, just a few minutes into the match, a visiting journalist turned to him and arrogantly asked, 'Is it me or is this the worst, but the worst, Northern Ireland team you've ever seen?' Darren muttered something about signs of improvement under Lawrie Sanchez, but the bloke just sneered. We all know, though, who had the last laugh.

It was smiles all round. David Beckham was grinning, most probably, at my stupidity; I, on the other hand, was smiling to hide my embarrassment. When you stop the England captain in the corridor and ask for an autograph, holding up the entire squad in the process, it pays to have some bloody ink in the pen. My nephew Shann Leahy had asked me to get Becks' signature, but it was a little awkward. I was at the game as a commentator, not a fan, so I felt obliged to act in a professional manner. This time, though, I was aware that it wasn't just anybody's autograph Shann was after. I had come down from my commentary position to a small room near the dressing-rooms. It's where I go over my research for the last time, nicking out occasionally to clarify facts with the players as they go out to warm up. So, nothing ventured, nothing gained. The door to the away dressing-room opened and, en masse, the England squad filed out. When David Beckham got to within a couple of feet of me, I stepped out and introduced myself: 'Mr Beckham, I'm Jackie from the BBC, I'm commentating on the match tonight. I just wondered if you would sign this quickly for a lad I know?' Becks smiled, swapped the ball to his other hand, took my pen and began to write. Nothing – the damned thing wasn't working. He smiled and tried again. Still the pen was as dry as a Bedouin's sandal. Much as I would have liked to hold up the England team for another couple of hours, I had no option but to thank him, apologise and rather sheepishly stand to one side. Not a good omen, you'd have to say.

The atmosphere inside Windsor Park was incredible, 14,000 sounding more like 140,000. Straight from the whistle it was clear the players were well and truly up for it, although it did take seven seconds for the game plan to kick in. That's how long it took James Quinn to commit the first foul of the match on Ashley Cole. Now, it wasn't that we were going to kick England around the park all night, but we were going to make it our type of tempo. At Old Trafford, we'd perhaps shown too much respect, given Gerrard and co. too much time on the ball. Repeat that mistake now, give them room to display their obvious skills, and Messrs Rooney, Beckham and Lampard might well cut us to pieces. We needed to persuade the Premiership stars to roll up their sleeves and participate in something a little less stylish. We wanted a good old-fashioned British game of football.

But it wasn't all backs-to-the-wall battling. There's a misconception, mostly on the English side it has to be said, that we scored one lucky goal and held on. That's only if you were looking at the game through red-rose-tinted glasses. Sure, Beckham sprayed some marvellous long-range passes, but they were from inside his own half. He did hit the post with a wicked free kick, but how many clear-cut chances were created? Michael Owen had perhaps the best opportunity, in the 45th minute with a close-range overhead kick. The Newcastle United striker connected cleanly enough, but his shot went straight to Maik Taylor. Lawrie Sanchez's half-time pep talk would have been markedly different had Owen's effort gone either side of the Birmingham keeper. It was the first time that I dared even consider that this might just be our night. Over the course of the match, though, there was little to choose between the teams in terms of goal-scoring opportunities. Conveniently forgotten are James Quinn's superb long-range drive, the delicate chip from David Healy that had Robinson scrambling and Warren Feeney's late strike, which was pulled just wide. In the end, it came down to one moment.

'Here's Davis, a good ball, the flag stays down . . . Healy!' I remember every moment of my commentary on the goal. The pregnant pause when it hit the net that made Linda, watching at home, fear that I'd had another seizure; Mike Edgar, my boss, who had only come into the commentary box a few moments before, yelping with delight; the deafening roar of the crowd before I continued, 'What a moment for Windsor Park, what a moment for Northern Ireland!' It was a goal good enough to win any game, engineered by Steve Davis with the deftest of passes, which was clinically dispatched by David Healy. It was one of those glorious 'I was there' moments. I had been fortunate that my broadcasting career had coincided with a halcyon era for Northern Ireland: two World Cups and stunning against-the-odds triumphs. I thought I'd had more than my fair share.

Everyone connected with Northern Ireland football went through the mill during those final 12 minutes of normal time. When the official held up his board to signal four minutes more, it became almost unbearable. We weren't going to be denied, though, and the Swiss referee brought an end to our agony. The noise on the final whistle was breathtaking; I'm surprised Windsor Park's creaking stands didn't just crumble like Jericho. There were no tears in my eyes as I described the jubilant scenes inside the old stadium, but I did think to myself, 'This, Jackie, is what it's all about.'

I learned a lot about myself that night, about just how far down the road to recovery I'd come. But that wasn't the only eye-opener. To borrow from Kipling (not the guy with the cakes, the one who penned exceedingly good poetry), 'If you can meet with Triumph and Disaster / And treat those two impostors just the same . . .' Well, 7 September 2005 was also the night David Beckham showed me he wasn't just a man, but one of real character. Despite the fashion shoots and designer endorsements, he retains an almost adolescent passion for the game. That's why he appreciated what this win meant to the Northern Ireland fans, why he paid tribute to them in his post-match interview. During England's warm-down after victory at Old Trafford, it was Beckham who led the applause for our travelling support. Sven's skipper was still mindful of the backing they'd give their team five months later, respectfully acknowledging the Green and White Army again as he walked out at Windsor Park. Most would have forgiven him for not repeating the gesture post-match. Yet, despite his obvious disappointment, that's exactly what he did. It didn't end there. In the mixed zone, he conducted a lengthy television inquest – sorry, interview – with Sky. Then it was the turn of national BBC. I was next, followed by UTV's Claire McCollum, then radio and finally the written press. At all times, he was courteous in his approach, magnanimous in his words. Media duties completed, Beckham could not have been criticised for seeking some solitude. However, unlike his teammates, who hurried, heads down, onto their coach, Beckham went to the fans. It was the first time since the superstars arrived that the public got close enough to ask for a prized autograph. It was the biggest star of the lot who signed them until security guards ushered him away.

'We're not Brazil, we're Northern Ireland, we're not Brazil, we're Northern Ireland. We're not Brazil, we're Northern Ireland, but it's all the same to me.'

In an effort to eradicate sectarianism, considerable time and effort went into writing new songs for the terrace faithful. None struck a chord in quite the same way as 'We're Not Brazil', a tongue-in-cheek tune that says a great deal about the men and women who follow their 'wee country'. You would never catch followers of 'Eng-ger-land' engaging in self-deprecating humour on the terraces. They take themselves too seriously. But that's exactly why they will never understand how good it felt to beat them. Only when you've been at your lowest point, been unable to buy a goal or steal a win, been the laughing stock of Europe, can you truly appreciate such highs. It's the same in life – my surgery taught me that.

Chapter Fourteen

MY WAY

I was waiting for John Terry to emerge from the changing-room. Chelsea's captain had promised to give us a few words about the club's youth-team coach, Brendan Rodgers. His manager, José Mourinho, had already given the man from Carnlough his seal of approval, and, with Terry's endorsement, our *Season Ticket* feature would be complete. I wasn't expecting anything other than a glowing report. I'd already seen enough in the few short hours we'd been filming to know they thought the world of him here. We'll be hearing a lot more about this likeable 32-year-old in the future. Intelligent, articulate, supremely self-confident, there's more than a little Mourinho about our man. Brendan left County Antrim as a teenager, dreaming of becoming a professional footballer. Five years later, that dream was over. Injury forced him to rethink, and, instead of coming home, Brendan merely readjusted his sights and became a coach. Specialising in nurturing talent at Reading, then a Championship side, he soon came to the attention of Chelsea. José Mourinho, only a few months into the job at Stamford Bridge, thought our Brendan 'special' enough to join his staff. Now clearly a respected figure within the Chelsea backroom, Brendan not only secured us access to the club's magnificent training ground in Cobham, Surrey, he also personally escorted us into the facility's inner sanctum.

You can tell it's where the Premiership high-rollers hang out by the cars. With brazen Bentley Continentals, brash Beamers, and more top-of-the-range Mercs than a company directors' car park, this place reeked of money, and lots of it. I've been around a few corners, met some famous folk, but even I was a little awestruck. Of course, my producer, cameraman and I did our level best to appear impervious to it all. We chatted casually with Joe Cole as he left for the day, nodded in the direction of Hernán Crespo like we were best buddies and smiled at a fresh-faced Frank Lampard. But let's be honest, it's not every day, even in this business, that you get to share the same rarefied air as the Premiership's finest. My interview with the self-styled Special One had gone like clockwork, Mourinho proving to be pleasant, polite and polished. He was also, as you'd expect, consummately cool and completely charming. Mind you, if it was the unexpected we were after, there wasn't long to wait. After José jumped into his car and left, just a few minutes before John Terry appeared in his designer duds, things got a little weird.

There was the sound of displaced gravel, and then a black Range Rover and a Mercedes raced into the enclosure. Doors were flung open, and out jumped half a dozen burly bodyguards. Not wanting to stare too long, I turned back to rejoin the conversation with Brendan, my producer and cameraman. As I did, I discovered a bloke standing in front of me with his hand out. Wearing scruffy-looking jeans, a tatty jumper, bomber jacket and trainers, it was none other than Chelsea's billionaire owner Roman Abramovich. The Russian shook each of our hands without uttering a word, then disappeared into the building. We looked at one another just to confirm it had happened, then, not wishing to fail to capitalise on such a chance encounter, we asked Brendan to see if we could take a few shots of Mr Abramovich as he was leaving. 'You shoot him and I'll shoot you' was the chief security advisor's pithy response. Then he pointed in my direction and shouted something. I didn't quite hear, but smiled and waved anyway. 'That fella knows you,' Brendan said when he returned. He'd been a British Army squaddie stationed in Northern Ireland during the early '80s. He remembered me as the bloke who read the sport.

This job and the people you meet doing it never cease to surprise. That's one of the reasons why I love it. John Terry is another classic example. I'd read the lurid tabloid headlines, the tales of nights out on the tiles, and I was convinced the England centre-half would be a cheeky, cocky cockney. I had the lad pegged all wrong. Brendan told me that Gianfranco Zola had taken Terry under his wing, turned his life around and transformed him into the model professional. He explained how Terry paid for the driving lessons of every apprentice at the club, how he always had time for the youth players. He recalled arriving at the training ground the morning after a Champions League match to find John enjoying a kickabout with his mates. 'You'll like John,' Brendan assured me. He was right. During our interview, the defender was on a charm offensive, his disarming manner scoring high marks with me. 'Rich and famous' can often translate as 'rude and fractious'. It's all the more refreshing, then, when money and celebrity fail to overpower the real person. Mind you, if there was a Premiership table for unpretentious players, I know a German who would give the Englishman a run for his money.

I first met the goalmeister, Jurgen Klinsmann, when Germany used the Blanchflower complex in Belfast as its base ahead of Euro '96. We spoke again following Northern Ireland's 3–1 loss to his country at Windsor Park in August 1997. By then, of course, I already knew that the blond-haired striker was, as Gary Mabbutt once called him, 'a very nice chap'. I had the pleasure of spending time with Klinsmann during his spell with Spurs. It was a two-day shoot, one day with the player who had arrived at White Hart Lane in the summer of '94, and the other with a Tottenham legend of a different vintage, our own Pat Jennings. Like John Terry on the training pitch with his pals, Klinsmann demonstrated an unquenchable appetite and love for the game. Like Terry, he felt obliged to pass on what he had learned to others. It was actually during filming with Pat that I noticed Jurgen with around 40 schoolchildren. Big Pat told me it was a question-and-answer session with kids, which Klinsmann conducted twice a week. During a lull in our Jennings shoot, Jurgen wandered over. 'You still here?' he enquired. In perfect English, one of four languages the German star is fluent in, he spoke to me of his admiration for Pat Jennings and everything he'd achieved. There wasn't a hint of sycophancy. Klinsmann eventually moved to America, settling near Huntington Beach, on the outskirts of Los Angeles. I jetted out to interview him for *Football Focus*, the trip reinforcing my opinion of him as one of the game's true gentlemen. I don't profess to be a friend, but it was nice that Jurgen remembered me when he returned to Belfast in 2005 for Northern Ireland's 125th anniversary friendly international with Germany. The national-team boss by that time, he wished me well with my recovery from illness.

Forging good working relationships is, of course, essential in my job. Breaking stories, that first big interview, the inside track – they don't tend to come the way of strangers. I've been lucky, with the likes of Bestie and Fergie, to have been able to form and foster an association that went beyond interviewer and interviewee. Trust is an important ingredient, together with knowing exactly where and when to call in a favour. There is an inherent danger, though, in fraternising with the famous. For the minute you take things for granted and forget you reside on different sides of the fence, you're asking for trouble.

Jack Charlton and I always got on well. Just as Bertie Peacock had filled Sir Alex in on my modest playing career, so Ian St John gave big Jack enough background info to ensure a modicum of respect. Any time I was at Republic of Ireland training, Jack would chip the ball over and challenge me to demonstrate my first touch. 'You never lose it,' he'd quip. In 1993, during the build-up to the World Cup qualifying group clash between Bingie's Northern Ireland and big Jack's Republic, tensions were running high. Bingham had promised payback for the chants of 'one team in Ireland' at Lansdowne Road during the first meeting, won 3–0 by the Republic. That defeat hurt Bingie, as had Jack's fairly disparaging pre-match remarks about Northern Ireland. He responded with a broadside in the media about Jack's use of the 'granny rule'. 'At least our team is of Irish extraction and our players are not mercenaries,' he said. The bad feeling between the two camps, combined with an escalation in sectarian violence north of the border, made a volatile situation positively incendiary. Add to this the facts that this was Billy Bingham's last match in charge and that the Republic needed only a point to qualify for the World Cup finals, and it's a surprise the whole thing didn't self-combust.

It was against this provocative backdrop that Terry Smyth and I travelled to one the Republic's training sessions in Drogheda. Big Jack gave us a warm welcome as usual, and nothing was too much trouble. Things were slightly less convivial when Jack and the boys arrived in Belfast, but when he stepped off the coach, there was still an outstretched hand and a 'How are you, Jackie?' We chatted briefly, and I asked if he would mind being our live guest on the pitch at about ten past six. With a glint in his eye, Jack looked at me and said, 'Weren't you down in Dundalk? You see that producer of yours [Terry], he wants everything. I'm up here to win a football match and qualify.' Off the big man went, leaving me trying to work out if he was seriously peeved or just taking the 'p'. Sure enough, about 60 seconds before I was to go on air, big Jack strides across the pitch to join me. Jack had come through for me again, and I had no reason to believe things would be any different during the summer of 1994 when we followed him to the USA.

It started well stateside, big Jack enveloping me in one of his trademark bear hugs, saying how delighted he was to see me and then giving his first World Cup finals interview. When Jack and I had finished chatting, Terry Smyth rubbed his hands and threw me a look that said, 'This is going to be sweet.' Things began to unravel a couple of days later when our cameraman was unable to make it in time for one of big Jack's press conferences. He finally arrived just as the presser was breaking up, and I went over to apologise to Jack and ask his permission to speak to the Republic's skipper, Andy Townsend. I managed to get the 'sorry for being late' bit out, but the moment I began 'I was wondering . . .' Jack just lost it. Off he went on a foul-mouthed tirade that would have made a trooper blush. He attacked the effing press, the fact that he never got an effing minute to himself, then, basically, he told me to eff off. Jack's second-in-command, Maurice Setters, a man I'd known for many years, looked as shocked as I did. 'What was that all about?' he asked. 'I thought you were supposed to be pals.' Later that evening, Terry, John Laverty, Jim Gracey and I travelled into Orlando together for a civic reception being held for Republic of Ireland management and officials. As we walked towards the door, big Jack came out and headed straight for me. As he shouted my name, I whispered to Terry out of the side of my mouth, 'What have I done now?' It says a lot about the character of the big Geordie that, in full view of everyone, he gave me a hug and said, 'I was out of order today, shouting at you the way I did, because you're one of my pals. I shouldn't have done that.'

Big Jack and Bingie almost came to blows at Windsor Park after the 1–1 draw that secured the Republic's passage to USA '94. They were both caught up in the prevailing mood that night. It was tribal, confrontational and quite ugly at times. Occasionally, sport can be a showcase for the worst this country of ours has to offer. Thankfully, more often than not, it rises above political and religious differences. How else can you explain a wee Protestant from the Unionist heartland of Ballymena being received with open arms at Croke Park? I've never tried to hide my background, my culture – why should I? Be yourself, that's a good rule of thumb, and leave your prejudices at the gate. During the late '70s, I was driven to a function at the Star Club in the nationalist enclave of the Ardoyne. I was more than a touch apprehensive; after all, the preconceived notion would have been one of Republican gunmen and sympathisers seated at every table. That night passed like any other gig, with hundreds of folk chatting away and asking for autographs. Many of them reminded me of my mum and dad, working-class folk with no axe to grind. Just like the people of the Shankill, they were not all bigoted, bitter and twisted. That was an era when Gaelic Games were struggling for media exposure. At UTV, we were only beginning to reflect the scale of support for Gaelic football and hurling. One of our first live matches was the Championship clash between the footballers of Down and Dublin. On commentary, believe it or not, Jackie Fullerton!

It was former chairman of the Down County Board, the amiable T.P. Murphy, who instigated this bizarre choice for a voice. Terry Smyth told me T.P. was keen that I should do it, although I had my reservations. During the week prior to the match, Terry and I went to Newry to promote Ulster

Television's coverage. I was happy enough to go along, as it gave me the opportunity to reason with T.P. 'As you know, it's not my culture and background,' I explained. 'I don't know the intricacies of the game, and, aside from that mercurial redhead Barney Rock, I would have problems identifying the players.' T.P. remained tight-lipped, so I delivered what I thought would be the *coup de grâce*: 'What you'll get is a soccer-style commentary.' That final point, so to speak, sealed my fate. 'Sure, Jackie, isn't that the reason I want you?' said Mr Murphy with a smile. 'Our boys talk too much.' Stitched up like a kipper. I did commentate on the match, and I would later present a Championship programme. I'm no expert, far from it; I'll leave that to the likes of Martin McHugh and Jarlath Burns. I can, though, appreciate the passion people have for Gaelic Games, the skill and commitment of the players, and the intoxicating drama they regularly produce. I am also proud to say, as a Prod from Harryville, that I feel comfortable walking into Casement, Clones or Croker.

We all want to be liked, especially us sensitive souls in television land. It's a well-known fact that our egos bruise more easily than a ripe peach. I'm no exception. But it's not just the pursuit of a pleasing review that has kept me trying to please. I believe we owe it to the general public to pose for pictures and sign autographs. As a boy of six or seven, I stood outside the dressing-rooms at Ballymena Showgrounds hoping one of my United heroes would stop and sign his name. I still remember the feeling of hurt, the abject disappointment, if they kept on walking. It's why I always take the time to sign. I'm also aware of my image. Not that I have something to live up to – more something to dispel. Humour, particularly of the self-deprecating variety, can help melt the hardest of hearts, and convince those who've bought into the television's Mr Cool persona that I'm really not that guy.

The ladies of Leeson Street in the Creggan estate know what

I mean. In April 2006, I went to Derry to shoot the remarkable story of local man Don Mullan, his lifelong obsession with England World Cup hero Gordon Banks and the book he's written on the subject. The crew and I arrived at the Mullan family home only to find Banksie's flight had been delayed for half an hour. There was no waiting around in the car, though, not with Sadie and the girls about. I was ushered into the house and made to feel as welcome as a long-lost relative. I posed for mobile-phone snaps, signed some autographs, drank a cup of char and ate ham baps in the kitchen. The neighbourhood could not have been more hospitable. I was flattered, and grateful, as I am towards every person who took the time to write a card or lick a stamp to send his or her best wishes when I lay in hospital. People like that, or my number-one fan, Omagh woman Gail Mann, deserve my respect. Mind you, not everyone thinks I'm the greatest thing since sliced pan loaf; in fact, my fiercest critic lives under the same roof.

Linda has always been the first to let me know where I've gone wrong. No stumble or mumble goes unnoticed: each inappropriate interview question is drawn to my attention, every fashion faux pas mercilessly highlighted. I trust her to be honest with me, to play devil's advocate. You need that. My sons, too, keep my feet on the ground. Like when I got a little carried away during the month-long tour just before Easter 2006 of the Rat Pack tribute show I was in. There I was thinking I looked pretty damn good impersonating Dean Martin in theatres up and down the country. The boys, though, were less impressed. They just saw it as another chance to give their old man a bit of stick. 'Dad, are there any other ways you can think of embarrassing us?'

Through it all, Linda has been the rock on which our family has been built. It hasn't always been easy, and I couldn't have done it without her. When I changed my career at the age of 30, there was a difficult period of readjustment. Gone was the nine-to-five Jackie, the one who was always home for tea. He was replaced by the always at meetings, dinners, prize-givings and evening matches Jackie. It did bring a bit of tension to the marriage, and I still harbour guilt about leaving Linda to cope with a full-time teaching job, bringing up the boys, washing, ironing, gardening and just about everything else. But that was the nature of my job. I was hustling to establish myself. After nine months, I did offer to pack it all in and return to accountancy. Linda, though, knew I would always look back and regret not giving it a real go. She wouldn't hear of it. Some of the toughest times were during the World Cups of '82 and '86, each necessitating a five-week stay away from home. The night after big Gerry's goal beat Spain, I spoke on the phone to a despondent Linda. She wanted Northern Ireland to win, of course, but she also knew it meant I would be away for another two weeks.

Later that evening, I received another call from County Antrim. This time it was Maurice O'Neill, editor of the *Ballymena Guardian,* and the man who taught me the basics of journalism. Maurice was penning a front-page story about me working at the World Cup finals. I told him that I was delighted for Bingie and the boys, the downside being another fortnight without seeing Linda and the boys. I was soon made to realise the privileged position I was in. Maurice, not a man to mince his words, cut me off in mid-sentence. 'Are you mad? What are you talking about? There are thousands of people over here who would give their right arm to be where you are.' There's a balancing act to be performed between working life and home, and I don't always get it right. In recent years, people have asked why I didn't go to the World Cup in Japan and Korea, or to Commonwealth or Olympic games. The truth is that I don't want to. I've had my time. Four World Cups (two with Northern Ireland and two with the Republic) isn't a bad return. I don't mind international trips, or even short tours, but I have neither the will, nor, I suspect, the stamina, for the long haul. So what does the future hold?

Arsène Wenger once wrote about being a 32-year-old player/manager in France. He said to a trusted confidant, 'When you think that I can't play at this level any more, tell me.' Six months later, his friend said, 'You can't play at this level any more.' Wenger never played another game. I hope I don't need to be told. We can all delude ourselves, but I believe that I will know when the time is right to hang up the mike for good. I do put off even considering the 'R' word, but I'm not an ostrich. I am aware that I cannot go on for ever. I also understand why I've been gradually sidelined; it's a young man's business, after all. That said, there is still, in my book, a place for a familiar face, a recognisable voice. I don't want to be some old fossil, clinging on to the last vestiges of my dignity. If I lost my commentator's eye, as I call it, then maybe it would be time to call it quits. But even now, if I find myself in the press-box at a match when I'm not working, I can still identify the goal-scorer in a flash. That's years of experience, that's your training – that's a commentator's eye. As things stand, I still have something to offer. George Best said he never replaced the buzz of playing. That was the showcase for his sublime talent. As I headed towards my 30th birthday and the end of my playing days, I wondered what I would do with my Saturdays. Television gave me a new career, an enjoyable lifestyle and the chance to stay involved in sport, particularly football. For that, I'll always be grateful. I still get up on a Saturday with the same enthusiasm I possessed as a player. I head to the ground early, mill about the dressing-rooms, enjoy the banter. I love the sound of clattering studs, the smell of embrocation in my nostrils, the sense of anticipation as kick-off approaches. I love being part of it.

Life's not about fame and wealth, it's about family and health. If you don't believe me, just ask Darren Clarke! I don't look too far ahead now. I suppose you could say that my way is now one day at a time. The end of my television career is near, of that I'm certain, but I'm not ready to take my final bow, to disappear behind the curtain. I'm enjoying the journey too much to take my leave just yet, and I know there are still a few more miles left in the tank. Will I ever witness another moment like Healy's hammered winner against England or big Gerry's Spanish stunner? Who knows? That's the beauty of sport. If I've one regret, it's that I no longer have the same vitality that took me skipping up the pitch in Valencia after Gerry. Then again, I'm still smiling, life's good, and, in the grand scheme of things, it's hardly worth a mention.

INDEX

INDEX

INDEX